May the Goo[d]

comfort and console yo[u]

Much love

Dr. Joseph[ine] x

"NEAR RESTFUL WATERS"

PSALM TWENTY THREE

REFLECTIONS

on

The Lord's my Shepherd

PSALM TWENTY THREE

An Urgent Call ...

... to LIVE

... for HIM!

First published in hardback in Great Britain, December 8th 2005

Nihil Obstat: Michael Jackson, S.T.L., Censor Deputatus
Imprimatur: John Hull, Vicar General,
Diocese of Arundel & Brighton

Cum Permissu Superiorum, D.H.S.

A catalaogue record of this book is available from the British Museum

ISBN   1 903623 22 7   Hard Back

Typeset in Souvenir 11pt: © Gerald Vann

Printed & Bound: The Bath Press, Bath, England

This book is dedicated

to

HELEN

with whom

I share

God's Love

in Community

The Bible Texts used in this book are from the Jerusalem Bible

CONTENTS

INTRODUCTION

THE TORRENTIAL DRENCHING!

This 'Shepherd' Book, on The 23rd Psalm, 'The Lord's my Shepherd', was inspired one Sunday morning at Mass in Turvey Abbey, Bedfordshire. I live in Olney, only 5 miles from this wonderful oasis.

On this particular morning, end of July 2005, I felt so 'filled' after Communion, that I was compelled to rush home and write immediately, (not even waiting for the end of Mass!)

The anointing came on me like a waterfall in full torrent after the rains. I arrived home, quite overwhelmed by my inner experience, went to our little chapel, exposed the Blessed Sacrament. I simply stayed there writing and praying this psalm.

It took one full week. Bed at 1.30 am. Up at 4.00 am. Awakened with new Scripture texts on my tongue! No time to eat!

I simply had to keep writing, till the flood subsided and the anointing passed. It was like a torrential drenching. During each day, I could only think of Psalm 23, the words never left me! I prayed them, lived them, breathed them, devoured them and they devoured me! I applied them to everything and everyone I met. I spoke of them to everyone who phoned! I suggested to all that they read this amazing Psalm

23 and then to write down what it meant to them. This psalm was my constant companion.

A very dear friend of ours, whom I thank profoundly, took up the idea of a book and skilfully produced what you hold preciously in your hand today. A magnificent feat! A gift to the Good Shepherd from the Good Shepherd and to all those called to read it.

I want to share it with you, so that you too will 'fall in love' with the Good Shepherd and sense His caring Presence for you everywhere you go. His love is so true, faithful and constant. It pursues you all your life; you cannot escape it!

I beg Him to lead you and heal you by His Word, which I know will console and comfort you at all times, inspiring you to live for Him! Why not start today? Why wait till tomorrow? You will never be sorry. The effect of Psalm 23 on your life will be tremendous. Believe and you will see! My love and prayers for you.

Josephine Walsh D.H.S.

P.S. ...And by the way, He told me everything! He needed this book in a hurry and it had to be beautiful for Him, with colour and gold edges! So there you are!

Josephine Walsh, D.H.S.,
13 Aspreys, Olney, Bucks, MK46 5LN

CHAPTER ONE

The Lord is my Shepherd,
there is
nothing I shall want.

(Psalm 23:1)

I SHALL NOT WANT!

ܠܕܘܝܕ. ܥܠ ܦܠܚܘܬܐ ܕܥܒܕܘܬܗ. ܘܥܠ ܗܘܐ
ܙܘܚܐܐܠܬ ܡܫܡܠܝܬܐ ܕܥܡܐ ܕܬܫܒܘܚܬܐ ܡܬܐܠܬ.
ܩܠܬ ܟܓ.

ܡܪܝܐ ܢܪܥܝܢܝ ܘܡܕܡ ܠܐ ܢܚܣܪ ܠܝ: *ܘܥܠ
ܡܪ̈ܥܝܬܐ ܕܬܕܐܐ ܢܫܪܝܢܝ. ܘܥܠ ܡܝ̈ܐ ܢܝܚܐ
ܢܕܒܪܢܝ: *ܢܦܫܝ ܐܦܢܝ ܘܕܒܪܢܝ ܒܫܒܝ̈ܠܐ
ܟܐܢܘܬܐ. ܡܛܠ ܫܡܗ *ܐܦ ܐܢ ܐܗܠܟ: ܒܛܠܠܝ
ܡܘܬܐ. ܠܐ ܐܕܚܠ ܡܢ ܒܝܫܬܐ ܡܛܠ
ܕܐܢܬ ܥܡܝ: ܫܒܛܟ ܘܚܘܛܪܟ ܗܢܘܢ ܒܝܐܘܢܝ.
ܠܥܠܡ ܕܥܠܡܝܢ

*ܛܝܒܬ ܩܕܡܝ ܦܬܘܪܐ ܠܘܩܒܠ ܒܥܠܕܒܒܝ:
ܐܦܫܬ ܒܡܫܚܐ ܪܫܝ ܘܟܣܝ ܪܘܐ ܐܝܟ ܚܝܠܐ.
*ܛܝܒܘܬܟ ܘܪܚܡܝܟ ܢܪܕܦܘܢܢܝ: ܒܟܠܗܘܢ ܝܘܡܬܐ
ܕܚܝܝ. ܘܐܥܡܪ ܒܒܝܬܗ ܕܡܪܝܐ ܠܐܘܪܟ ܝܘܡܬܐ:

This is the Aramaic version of the 23rd Psalm which Jesus would have used at home praying with his parents, Mary and Joseph, as a child in Nazareth.

I SHALL NOT WANT!

Yahweh is my Shepherd,
I lack nothing.
In meadows of green grass he lets me lie.
To the waters of repose He leads me;
there He revives my soul.

He guides me by paths of virtue
for the sake of his name.

Though I pass through a gloomy valley,
I fear no harm;
beside me Your rod and Your staff
are there, to hearten me.

You prepare a table for me
under the eyes of my enemies;
You anoint my head with oil,
my cup brims over.

Ah, how goodness and kindness
pursue me, every day of my life;
my home, the house of Yahweh,
as long as I live!

(Jerusalem Bible)

Psalm Twenty Three

There is hardly a better known and loved image of God in Sacred Scripture than that of the Good Shepherd. The Shepherd theme weaves in and out of Salvation History, beginning with the Old Testament, till we come to its fulfilment in Jesus Christ, the Son of God, born of Mary, the Immaculate Virgin Mother of God, of the House of David, the Saviour, the One sent from the Father.

In St. John's Gospel, chapter 10, we find Jesus identifying Himself with the Shepherd of the Old Testament, qualifying His own title as 'The Good Shepherd' in the New Testament. He continues by telling us that He is the One who gives His Life for His sheep; the One to whom the sheep belong.

The psalmist cries:
"Shepherd of Israel, listen, You who lead
Joseph like a flock; enthroned on the
cherubs, shine on Ephraim, Benjamin and
Menasseh; rouse Your strength, come to us
and save us! Yahweh Sabaoth bring us back,
let Your face smile on us, and we shall be
safe. *(Psalm 80:1-3)*

Jesus claims to be this same Shepherd of
Israel, but more. He Himself says:
"I am the Good Shepherd. The sheep that
belong to Me listen to My voice. I know
them, and they follow Me. I give them
Eternal Life. They will never be lost. And
no one will ever steal them from Me. The
Father who gave them to Me is greater than
anyone. And no one can steal from My
Father. The Father and I are one."
(John 10:14, 27-30)

This amazing claim: 'The Father and I are
One,' tells us of Jesus' unity with God,
through the perfect love of Son and Father,
and Jesus' perfect obedience to the Father,
through His Oneness of Heart with the
Father.

We read in Scripture that:
"Jesus is the image of the unseen God and

the first-born of all creation, for in Him
were created, all things in Heaven and on
Earth; everything visible and invisible;
Thrones, Dominations, Sovereignties,
Powers- all things were created through
Him and for Him. Before anything was
created, He existed, and He holds all things
in unity. Now the Church is His Body, and
He is the Head." *(Colossians 1:15-20)*
Our faith tells us that there are three
Persons in one God, the Father, the Son,
and the Holy Spirit, called The Blessed
Trinity. Jesus' claim to be 'One with the
Father' makes Him equal to God. This is
the mystery of our faith, which we accept
and believe as Christians. Jesus Himself
being our teacher.

Jesus tells us that: 'No one can come to the
Father except through Him.' *(John 6:37)*
He has told us that He is the 'Only' image
of God the Father.
"Not that anyone has seen the Father,
except the One who comes from God: He
has seen the Father." *(John 6:46)* Jesus is
speaking of Himself of course!
Jesus has also told us, that to see Him, is to
see the Father: "To have seen Me, is to
have seen the Father," Jesus said to Philip.
(John 14:9).

"No one has ever seen God; it is the only
Son, who is nearest to the Father's heart,
who has made Him known". *(John 1:18)*
Jesus again speaking of Himself.

Jesus is the Centre of the Universe. He is
the sum total of Salvation History and He is
the Bridge between Earth and Heaven. He
is Everything. He, Jesus, is the revealed
Truth. *(John 14:6)* He is the Only
Begotten Son of God; The Chosen One;
The Beloved Son, on whom the Father's
favour rests and in whom He is well
pleased! *(cf. Matthew 3; Luke 9; Mark 9; John1).*
Such mysteries! What revelation!
We can only bow down and adore. Faith is
such a gift that can never be equalled. It
cannot be explained. It cannot be earned
or bought. It is total free Gift. Such
mystery is beyond comprehension. What a
privilege for us to know and believe! Thank
you, Lord. Increase our faith.

Psalm Twenty Three, known as 'The Good
Shepherd' psalm, is prophetic in content. It
is perfect in word and expression. It is a
masterpiece of poetry and song, lacking
nothing. It never grows old. It gives
exquisite representation of God, as the
Good Shepherd, leading His sheep to rich

pastures, green and lush, beside restful waters, where they can be safe and without fear, close to the Good Shepherd.

The sheep will be shepherded by Him from attack, and with His crook and His staff, He will rescue any of His sheep that might go astray. Such a beautiful and complete psalm, set to music with many different versions, sung on all occasions, and appropriate to every occasion, whether it be wedding, baptism, funeral, or jubilee. Nothing can eclipse its beauty and eternal quality. It expresses in great depth, what everyone can understand, whether they are religious or not.

The words are so endearing, comforting, that they never lose their richness and appeal, whether recited or sung. To recite this psalm and meditate on it, brings peace to the soul and such a sense of wholeness to one's being, that I find it really is better than any tonic! The words have an extraordinary power.

To use even the opening sentence as a mantra, repeating the words over and over again, is better than gold. It's like medicine. Its richness seeps into the soul like a refreshing dew, making you feel refreshed and 'at home' with the Good Shepherd, where you can be yourself and be part of His flock. Any sense of isolation or loneliness disappears, for when you are with the Good Shepherd, it's hard to focus on yourself. His Presence is so all absorbing. Each sheep He calls by name, each sheep is precious to Him, that He says even if He lost one, He would have to go after it, and leave the ninety nine that have not gone astray.

"And when He found it, would He not joyfully take it on His shoulders and then when He got home, call together His friends and neighbours? 'Rejoice with Me', He would say, 'I have found My sheep that was lost.' In the same way, I tell you there will be more rejoicing in Heaven over one repentant sinner, than over ninety-nine virtuous men who have no need of repentance." *(Luke 15:4-7)*

Such is the delight of God's Word which is balm to the soul. "I devoured Your words when they came. They were my happiness and I felt full of joy when You made Your Name rest on me." *(Jeremiah 15:16)*

The Good Shepherd always gives another chance for his sheep to come home to Him. When God's Words are given a chance they become 'alive and active, cutting finely like a double edged sword, slipping through the places where the soul is divided from the spirit.' *(Hebrews 4:12)* God's Word challenges us to unity, peace, conversion and new life.

If you use psalm twenty three often, try for yourself and see its effect on your life. It is pure nourishment. Simply read the psalm through slowly, meditatively. The words will come alive for you and before you know where you are, you're in the company of the Good Shepherd, in soft green pastures, where He is giving you repose, peace and joy. Pray it like this, then take a sheet of paper and write your thoughts. Lovely! Healing!

I love the image of the Good Shepherd Host, who invites His guests to His table, anointing their heads with oil, filling their cups to overflowing, while at the same time lavishing them with goodness and kindness, as they dwell in His house forever. It is God's munificence, and magnanimity, described here so beautifully.

I live with Sr. Helen in religious community, and we so often say how incredibly generous our God is to us, and has been to us all our lives, that we wonder how we can ever repay His goodness to us, and so with the psalmist, overwhelmed as we are, we often cry out: "How can I repay the Lord for His goodness to me?" *(Psalm 116:12)*

We have certainly received from Him, throughout our lives, much more than the hundredfold He promised to those who leave all to follow Him in Religious Life. If we spend our whole life in thanking Him, it would not be enough. How can anyone find words to thank Him! How can anyone repay Him, the Giver of all. Never!

My wonderful godchild, Christine Scotcher, was so overpowered by the grace of God after her Baptism at Turvey Abbey, (Easter 1994 at 4 am!) that she did not know how to contain her joy and excitement during the days that followed her reception into the Catholic Church. She used to ring up sometimes and say: "What can I do?" "How can I repay the Lord for His goodness to me? The cup of salvation I will take up. I will call on the Lord's name." *(Psalm 116:12-14)*

I Shall Not Want!

The sheer joy of knowing the Lord, this newness of life, this 'living faith', this richness and abundance, or should I say, super abundance of love, (like a rushing stream when the water is in full spate) this newness of church community, (inheriting many more friends, and 'faith', brothers and sisters) Christine found overwhelming.

As an extra special bonus, she was soaked in the wonderful 'Benedictine' spirituality of Turvey Abbey, Bedfordshire, where, with St. Benedict as patron of the Benedictine nuns and monks, she can frequently join in the prayer of the church, (her great love), chanting the psalms whenever she can, at Matins, Lauds, Vespers and Compline.

Her non-catholic husband, Philip, is so gracious to allow her this liberty! The anointing of the Holy Spirit on her life, combined with her childlike response to God, made her cry out in praise to bless His holy name, forever. Her happiness could not be bought. It is pure gift from above, as is every gift from Him. "The Lord is My Shepherd, there is nothing I shall want." *(Psalm 23)*. In Him we are complete! And so, nothing on earth compares with the gift of faith.

What God is there like our God? What God
is so great as our God?
"You are a God who did marvellous things
and forced the nations to acknowledge Your
power, with your own arm redeeming your
people." *(Psalm 77:13)*

We, too, chant in chorus with the psalmist,
we want to tell the whole world of His
mighty deeds, of his mighty arm at work
and we are glad of every opportunity to
proclaim His greatness. "The Lord has
done marvels for us, holy is His name".
(Luke 1:49) Magnificat!

Let us return to Psalm Twenty Three, the
most loved psalm with such universal
appeal. Everyone can claim it as their own
personal prayer, alone or at a service, in
times of sadness or happiness, it seems to
make no difference but fits every occasion
perfectly, and at all times. The more you
pray this psalm, the more your mind
becomes filled with light, with goodness,
with noble thoughts! Try it! Psalm Twenty
Three cuts across creed, race, colour,
nationality, touching to the very roots of
being itself. I find it amazing. I have been
praying it much more lately and I am
experiencing a change in myself as a result!

Notice how, as you read it, the psalmist becomes aware of God, not as a 'He', but as a 'You'. The opening stanza or even first line, is, as it were a statement of who God is, and we talk of God as 'He'.

"The Lord is my Shepherd, there is nothing I shall want, fresh and green are the pastures where 'He' gives me repose". I notice that the words of the psalm become more 'personal', more applicable to the individual, and to the daily struggles when evil attacks.

"If I should walk in the valley of darkness, no evil would I fear", and so we find after this sentiment is expressed, the psalmist changes from talking of God as 'He' to addressing God as 'You', thus making the Good Shepherd the 'Personal' God for each sheep. From this moment the relationship changes, and the Good Shepherd takes on a new role for each one of His sheep.

'You' are there with 'Your' crook and 'Your' staff, with these 'You' give me comfort. 'You' meaning 'My' personal God; 'My' Shepherd, 'My' Deliverer, 'My' Redeemer, 'My' Saviour, 'My' Protector, 'My Rock', 'My' Home, 'My' Everything, and so the Good Shepherd becomes my Personal Saviour.

I need fear no evil for 'You are with me'.
You are always there to protect me. Even
darkness and death should not trouble me,
for You are there. You have prepared a
place for me in Your Kingdom where I can
dwell in Your House forever... And so, the
psalm becomes a treasured personal prayer
for each individual to use for themselves at
any time. There is an eternal flavour to it.

Neither need I fear for the Church, Christ's
living Body on Earth, to which His sheep
belong, because the Good Shepherd
promised He would be with His Church till
the end of time. "And know I am with you
always; yes, to the end of time."
(Matthew 28:20)
There can be no fear then, when thieves
and brigands try to break in and steal, for
Jesus says, "The sheep take no notice of
them." *(John 10:8)*
Again He says, when He made Peter the first
Pope and the Head of the Church:
"You are Peter, and upon this rock I will build
My Church, and the gates of the underworld can
never hold out against it." *(Matthew 16:18-19)*

St. Peter, following in the Good Shepherd's
footsteps, as the first chosen Shepherd of
the sheep after Jesus, has a word for all the

shepherds in line after him, until the Church is no more:

"Be the Shepherds of the Flock of God that is entrusted to you: watch over it; not simply as a duty but gladly, because God wants it; not for sordid money, but because you are eager to do it. Never be a dictator over any group that is put in your charge, but be an example that the whole flock can follow. When the Chief Shepherd appears, you will be given the crown of unfading glory." *(1 Peter 5:3-4)*

The Catholic Church loves the Psalms and uses them constantly in her liturgy. We find she interprets Psalm 23, 'The Lord is my Shepherd' in a very special way, seeing it as a hymn to the Seven Sacraments of the Church. These are seven very special channels of grace and of 'living' water, left to the Church by the Good Shepherd Himself, to feed His Flock. They are the life-blood of the church, the mainstay with the Holy Sacrifice of the Mass, and are epitomized in a very special way in this complete Psalm 23 'The Lord is My Shepherd'.

In the light of this amazing psalm, the Church interprets the Seven Sacraments as follows:

1) **Baptism :** 'Restful waters to revive me'

2) **Confirmation :** 'Led on the right path'

3) **Communion :** 'Prepared a table for me'

4) **Reconciliation:** 'You are there with Your crook and Your staff'

5) **For the Sick :** 'Though I walk in the valley of darkness'

6) **Holy Orders :** 'My head You have anointed with oil'

7) **Marriage :** 'Surely goodness and kindness shall follow me'

The complete collection of all the one hundred and fifty psalms is called 'The Psalter', containing themes ranging from deep sorrow for sin to great heights of joy and happiness and trust in God; from a cry in deep distress, where one is up to one's neck in trouble *(Psalm 69:1-2)* to praising God with thanksgiving, *(Psalms 149 &150)* to repentance for sin.

The great King David, poet, hymn-writer, musician, wrote most of the psalms. He was the national poet of the Hebrews, known as Israel's beautiful psalmist. It was he who cried out to God, in that classic and well loved psalm 50, 'The Miserere', which he wrote after He had publicly sinned and let himself and His Maker down so badly, as we do sometimes!!

"Have mercy on me, God, in Your kindness.
In Your compassion, blot out my offence.
O, wash me more and more from my guilt
And cleanse me from my sin…" *(Psalm 50:1-2)*

Why not take this psalm and pray it through quietly for yourself. We are all sinners before Him. It may help you to write your thoughts.

The Curé d'Ars, that dear old saint of the Catholic church, mystic and priest, who was given by God an amazing grace of knowing peoples' sins even before they confessed them, (so they couldn't get away with any!) and to whom people came from all over the world for confessions, wrote of David and the psalms: "When I think of the beautiful psalms, I am tempted to cry out, 'O Happy

Fault !' for if David had had no sin to
lament, we should be all the poorer and be
without the psalms today." From the
psalms, the Curé's love passed on to the
very book that contained them, his breviary,
which he loved so much, and which he took
with him everywhere he went.

The Catholic church loves the Psalter. She
places great emphasis and value on the
psalter, suggesting its use daily in prayer.
The prayer life of Religious Orders is very
much founded on the psalms, as is
especially the prayer of the enclosed orders,
like the Cistercians at Mount St. Bernard's
Abbey, Leicestershire or Caldey Island, off
the coast of South Wales.

The monks rise at 3 a.m. daily to pray and
chant the psalms in the Divine Office in
communal prayer, so if you can't sleep,
remember these wonderful monks are up
already praying for you and for the world.
They actually pray a selection of the psalms
seven times a day.
The Church at Rome instituted the public
recitation of the psalms at the Canonical
Hours of Prayer (Monastic life!) and so the
psalms are chanted, usually beautifully, by
the monks and nuns in community prayer

daily. Visiting monasteries at prayer time is quite a treat, and often outsiders can join in these prayers too. There is somehow a heavenly aura about it all. There is a peace the world cannot give. The psalms are used for private prayer as well as public prayer, just as they were used in the time of Jesus. I personally love to use the psalms a lot in my prayer, as I do love them dearly, and find them so inspirational.

We find Jesus Himself as a child, would have been praying the psalms daily in His own language *(Aramaic)*, with His mother Mary and Joseph at the holy house of Nazareth, where he lived with them, and His prayer book would have been the psalter.

All true Israelites used the psalter as their hymn book. Jesus would have been no exception. He would have recited the processional psalms on His way up to Jerusalem with His parents and, of course, would have used many other psalms in the Temple and Synagogue, even those foretelling His very own suffering and death! The apostles, early Christians, early Desert Fathers and early Christian martyrs, would all have been familiar with the

psalms. Jesus Himself explained the psalms
to the two disciples on the way to Emmaus
after His Resurrection. They were worried
about the recent happenings in Jerusalem
about His horrendous death thinking He
was dead, when, to their surprise, He came
up, incognito, and walked beside them and
told them that everything written in the
psalms and prophets about Himself was
fulfilled in Himself.

These two disciples would have known the
psalms, and so when Jesus recalled for
them things they would have already read
about, especially about the Messiah, it
would have rung a bell for them. If not
immediately, their eyes would have been
opened as their hearts burned within them.
The psalms are God's Word, and so they are
alive, real, and true, and they do help our
hearts to burn within us in response to His
Word. There's nothing stale about the
psalms, nor could there ever be.

The psalmist wrote: "With the harp I will
solve my problems." *(Psalm 49:4)* I can
almost hear the Israelites chanting this, as
they walked along, assuring themselves that
God is in charge in spite of all their
difficulties. Somehow this verse does make

sense, for the psalms were often sung with stringed instruments, and music certainly does have a power to soothe and heal. In fact, I know a wonderful physiotherapist who so often sings and hums to his patients, as he has discovered the immense power of music in healing. I have just bought a book called the Mozart Effect, which claims healing through listening to Mozart's music. I can't wait to read it, as I am a great fan of Mozart and I used to love playing his piano sonatas and his clarinet music too. So I may have a lovely surprise in store for me!

The Israelites would have chanted these psalms in the fields as they dressed the vines and harvested the crops and, like the good old Irish people on the land, God was never far from them. In sorrow and in joy the Israelites used the psalms, for the psalms plumb the depth of human emotions from the heights to the depths. Some of the psalms are shockingly frank with God, with cries that pierce to the heart, even crying out revenge on their enemies! "God, break their teeth in their mouths, Yahweh wrench out the fangs of the savage lions!" *(Psalm 58:8)* Heavy stuff isn't it? And there's even worse!

When I was a teenager in Limerick, I had a
school friend, who entered the Convent
with me, and who is now one of our nuns!
She had the funniest of expressions, and so
did her mother. One of these weird
expressions was "I'll break your face in" if
you teased her or said something she did
not approve of. Now she certainly didn't
mean that literally. We'd all laugh and tell
her to stop saying those awful things. But
perhaps the psalmist was just as expressive!

There's nothing like these funny sayings. I
know 'at home', we had several of them and
had many a laugh with my mom and dad!
Also, I noticed Limerick people have sayings
all of their own like no where else, and other
people don't understand them. Unless you
were a Limerick person you just wouldn't
understand them. You'd probably think we
were terrible! It may even be the same with
the psalmist, who knows that God
understands. "Listen to my cry for help, I can
hardly be crushed any lower." *(Psalm 142)*

David wasn't ashamed in Psalm 69 to cry out
to God aloud, probably after his 'big' sin:–
"Save me, God! The water is already up to
my neck! I am sinking in the deepest
swamp, there is no foothold, I have slipped

into deep water and the waves are washing over me. Worn out with calling, my throat is hoarse, my eyes are strained, looking for my God." *(Psalm 69:1-2)*

We may be too polite to speak to God like this! We're so respectable, but David turns to God in sorrow, weeping: "My sin is always before me: blot out all my sins: I have sinned constantly in mind, having sinned against none other than You, having done what You regard as wrong… Wash me until I am whiter than snow." *(Psalm 50:2-4,7)* And God gives David a new start.

John Newton (1725-1807), vicar of the Anglican Church in Olney, Buckinghamshire, (where I live), had once been a nasty slave trader. In a similar way to David, he, too, had sinned publicly and after his conversion wrote his conversion hymn, 'Amazing Grace' in the rectory attic.

This, like David's psalm 50, was his act of sorrow to God. So this hymn could, I suppose, be considered a modern day psalm. Now, it is of worldwide renown, sung on all occasions, touches many hearts, often moves people to tears. It is a very healing hymn.

My brother -in-law, Denis, in South Africa wrote to me and called it 'my' hymn. He told me in a wonderful letter, after he had

© *Photograph Josephine Walsh*

had his heart attack, that when he came back to church, having been away for years, they were singing 'my' hymn 'Amazing Grace'. It brought healing to him, too. "It's thanks to your prayers and your mother's prayers", he wrote, "that God gave me a second chance". After this he couldn't pray enough, couldn't go to Mass enough, couldn't love God enough, bless him! God really touched his spirit and gave him many more years to enjoy his love, before calling him home to be with Him.

This shows the power of intercessory prayer, for, unknown to him, I had prayed for him often over the years. So never give up praying for people.

In case you would like to sing or pray this lovely hymn, I include the words here for you.

Amazing grace! How sweet the sound that saved a wretch like me. I once was lost, but now I'm found, was blind, but now I see.

'Twas grace that taught my heart to fear and grace my fears relieved. How precious did that grace appear the hour I first believed.

Through many dangers, toil and snares I have already come. 'Tis grace hath brought me safe thus far and grace will lead me home.

The Lord has promised good to me;
His Word my hope secures;
He will my shield and portion be
as long as life endures.

When we've been there ten
thousand years
bright shining as the sun;
We've no less days to sing God's
praise
Than when we first began.
(John Newton 1725-1807)

Why not stop just now and write a poem, a song, or some prose, of God's goodness to you throughout your life. I'm sure you have so much for which to thank Him. You might surprise yourself! Glorify Him through it!

Overall, there is such a great variety of psalms. Some psalms are of praise, others of thanksgiving, trust, hope, adoration. One third are of petition (we are always asking), some are instructive, others are encouraging. Others again help us to adhere to God's Law, from which we reap the fruits of God's Kingdom while we're here on earth. These fruits would be the

virtues like love, joy, peace, faithfulness,
kindness, goodness, forgiveness, chastity,
harmony, unity, faith, gentleness,   etc.

The psalms, I find, to be very vivid prayers,
and with a little bit of imagination, they can
help us to 'wake up' to God, on our
spiritual journey. They bring great benefit
of healing, comfort, motivation, and musical
enjoyment.

I think they really should be sung. I used to
love the Gelineau rendering of the psalms,
so tuneful and easy to sing and memorise,
with their lovely antiphons. Quite 'catchy'
tunes that you could sing during the day to
yourself! It is such a shame that they are
not used much today. I find many churches
do not sing the responsorial psalm on a
Sunday at Mass. This is such a shame, as
the psalm is really supposed to be sung.

Unfortunately sometimes, when it is sung,
the setting is so boring musically, that it is a
pity for the congregation. Something
definitely needs to be done about the psalm
at Mass. Maybe, a little extra time could be
given to preparation of the liturgy, to
choose a more melodic setting, with the

music better suiting the words, and a tuneful response, that everyone would enjoy singing. It would of course be such a contrast to the readings.

The psalms can express our correct attitude of reverence and adoration to God our Creator and Maker.

"Come in, let us bow and bend low.
Let us kneel before the God who made us,
for we are His People, the Flock that is led
by his hand." *(Psalm 95:6-7)*
We must never lose our sense of reverence for God. Remember, Moses had to take his shoes off in God's presence. Try to acquire the stillness that leads to adoration.

The central figure in the psalms is of course, Christ, the One longed for throughout the ages, the One who reigns above all Nations, the Messiah, the Anointed One.
David, a brilliant musician, would lead his people to proclaim Him, as he conducted his orchestra of harp, lutes, timbrels, cornets, and cymbals. *(2 Kings 6:5)*
Throughout the latter part of the Old Testament, David was recognised as the promoter of Israel's chant.

The exalted Messianic psalms (foretelling Jesus) present the anointed Son of Yahweh:–

'He will rule over the World'. *(Psalm 2:8)*
'He is a King: He rules from Mount Zion.' (viz. Heaven) *(Psalm 48:11)*

'His throne will remain forever.' *(Psalm 45:6)*
'He shares Yahweh's throne.' *(Psalm 2:7)*
'His reign will bring justice and peace; all Kings and Nations will worship Him. Tribes of the earth are blest by Him, He shall reign until the sun and moon are no more.' *(Psalm 72:5,11)*
'He is a priest of the order of Melchizedek' *(Psalm 109:4)*

"From the rising to the setting of the sun His name will be praised forever." *(Psalm 113:2-3)* Yet, this One, this anointed One, the Ruler of nations, whom tribes must worship, will undergo terrible sufferings *(Isaiah 53)*; becoming a worm rather than a man *(Psalm 22:6)*; digging nails into His hands and feet *(John 19:18)* and standing staring at His crucified body.

This is the Servant King, the One who will save Israel, the Suffering Servant, the Holy One of Israel, the Saviour, Jesus the

Redeemer, the Good Shepherd.
He declares:
"Mine is not a Kingdom of this world.
If My kingdom were of this world,
My men would have fought to prevent
My being surrendered to the Jews.
But My kingdom is not of this kind."
"So you are a king, then?" said Pilate.
"It is you who say it," answered Jesus.
"Yes, I am a King. I was born for this, I
came into the world for this: to bear
witness to the truth; and all who are on the
side of truth listen to My voice."
(John 18:36-37)

'A world-wide assembly, including rich and
poor, will pay homage to Him and will
partake of a sacrificial meal in His honour'.
(Psalm 22:25-26)

He is the Anointed One, the Christ, the
Messiah, the One foretold, the Lamb that
was slain. Jesus, the Lord, the Good
Shepherd, is the Anointed One Of God,
who fulfilled all that was written of Him in
the Scriptures.

'It is He who is coming on the clouds;
everyone will see Him, even those who
pierced Him, and all the races of the Earth

will mourn over Him. This is the Truth.
Amen. "I am the Alpha and the Omega,"
says the Lord.' *(Revelation 1:-7)*

'The Beginning and the End. I will give the
water from the well of life to anybody who
is thirsty, it is the rightful inheritance of the
One who proves victorious; and I will be His
God, and he a son to Me.' *(Revelation 21:6-7)*

"The Angel showed me the river of life,
(symbol of the Holy Spirit) rising from the
throne of God and the Lamb, and flowing
crystal clear, down the middle of the city
street. On either side of the river were
trees of life and the leaves of which are the
cure for the pagans.
The ban will be lifted. The Throne of God
and of the Lamb will be in its place in the
City; His servants will worship Him. They
will see Him face to face, and His name will
be written on their foreheads. It will never
be night again and they will not need
lamplight or sunlight, because the Lord will
be shining on them. They will reign forever
and ever. Happy are those who treasure
the prophetic message of this book."
(Revelation 22:1-7)

And so, to round off the first stanza of
David's wonderful psalm 'The Lord is My

Shepherd, there is nothing I shall want', I
would like to thank the psalmists who gave
us such rich prayers. We, like David, know
that there is nothing like knowing the Lord,
and there's nothing better than knowing His
love for you and even better still believing in
it. "Your love is better than life itself."
(Psalm 63:3)

If you take Psalm twenty three to heart, I
have no doubt that in a short time, you will
see dramatic changes in your attitude to life.
You will experience a depth in your
spirituality never known before and a sense
of God's Presence, and in your life there
will be 'nothing you will want' for 'The
Good Shepherd' will become your *all*.
Your 'in love' relationship with Him will
have begun.

When you know you're loved by someone
and most especially by God, what else is
there to know. When you see the effect of
love on people, you can rejoice and give
thanks. Isn't this what the world needs
most? When you see a faithful couple who
have loved each other for years through
'thick and thin', then what can you say but
marvel at the beauty of love, given and
received, and where there are children as
part of that love, what a bonus!

When you have a faithful friend who loves
you and who never lets you down, you
don't need to see each other all the time but
the fact that someone is constant, stable in
their love for you, loving you just as you
are, believing in you and delighting in your
friendship, you can grow tall, keep serene
and not doubt yourself and so help others
to grow tall too! Praying daily for every
person in the world to have a good friend,
is one way of spreading love. Why not take
on this intercession now. Start today!

If only we could grasp the truth, that God in
Jesus is our best friend. Our Beloved Good
Shepherd, our forever unchanging friend,
will never let us down. He can never 'not'
love us. " I have loved you with an
everlasting love and I am constant in my
affection for you." *(Jeremiah 31:3)* He will
always believe in us, He will always give us
another chance, use us, (even when we are
in bits!) hope in us, wait for us, ennoble us,
encourage us, enable us. When you believe
you're loved, everything begins to happen
for you. Love has a power all of its own.
Love is God. "God is Love." *(1 John 4:8)*

Life is for love. Let love alone be the
mainstay of all your actions. Always see

love as the source of everything that comes
from God.

When teaching, I noticed our sixth formers
changed when someone loved them, they
even produced better work while 'walking
on air' at being so loved and so special to
another human being.
Our friend, Jesus, not only showed us love
by 'taking on' our human nature and
becoming man like us (in everything but sin)
but He also died for us, so that from that
day, we would have eternal life, and want
for nothing. "A man can have no greater
love than to lay down His Life for His
Friends." *(John 15:13)*

Not many of us could love another to that
extent! Yet that's what the Good Shepherd
did for us. He gave His life for his sheep.
He died that we might live. He came that
each one of His sheep might have Eternal
Life. *(John 10:10)* In Him, we want for
nothing. Lord, I thank You with all my
heart. I want to love You forever. "Your love
will comfort Me for all the hatred. The more
you love, the more you will want to love.
Set aside a quarter of an hour a day for
love, for nothing else but love." *('He and I',
Gabrielle Bossis, p.228)*

"Yes, Jesus is enough. Where He is,
nothing is missing; Jesus is Master of the
impossible.
One of the things we absolutely owe to Our
Lord is never to be afraid. For the
proclamation of the Holy Gospel, I am ready
to go to the ends of the earth and live to the
end of time.
Live as if you were to be martyred today!"
('Silent Pilgrimage', Charles de Foucauld, p.24)

It is amazing, how the Lord took Charles de
Foucauld at his word, hearing his prayer to
die a martyr. This was his deepest desire to
which he often referred in prayer, to die for
Jesus, his beloved friend. Jesus, the Good
Shepherd, gave His life for him, so Charles,
like so many others wanted to give his life
for Jesus. He was granted his wish. He
was martyred on 1st December 1916.

"The Lord is my Shepherd there is nothing
I shall want." *(Psalm 23:1)*

And so, this well loved psalm sums up the
whole of Salvation History. We are
reminded of the Israelites forty years
wandering in the desert, the manna God
sent them as food from heaven, the water
of refreshment from the rock, the steadfast

hope in God the Shepherd, the struggle for the Promised Land, the faithfulness of God and His constant care and protection from enemies, His constant Presence, and the security of dwelling in His House forever.

The Good Shepherd reminds us: "There are many rooms in My Father's house; if there were not, I should have told you. I am going now to prepare a place for you, and after I have gone and prepared you a place, I shall return to take you with Me; so that, where I am, you may be too. You know the Way to the place I am going." *(John 14:2-4)*

And by the way, did you know that God is Eternal. He has no beginning, He will never end. No one created Him. He is the eternal 'I Am'.

He is your Good Shepherd. With Him you will never want. He is always surprising us and will surprise us to the end and after. Trust your life fully to Him. You will never regret it.

PSALM TWENTY THREE

CHAPTER TWO

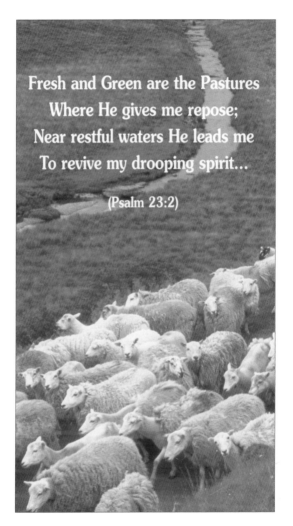

Fresh and Green are the Pastures
Where He gives me repose;
Near restful waters He leads me
To revive my drooping spirit...

(Psalm 23:2)

HE GIVES ME REPOSE!

PSALM TWENTY THREE

The Lord is my Shepherd,
There is nothing I shall want.
Fresh and green are the pastures
Where He gives me repose,
Near restful waters He leads me
To revive my drooping spirit.

He guides me along the right path
He is true to His name.
If I should walk in the valley of
darkness
No evil would I fear.
You are there with your crook
and your staff
With these you give me comfort.

You have prepared a banquet for me
In the sight of my foes.
My head you have anointed with oil,
My cup is overflowing.

Surely goodness and kindness
shall follow me
All the days of my life.
In the Lord's own house shall I dwell
Forever and ever.   Amen.

PSALM 23 – With Antiphons

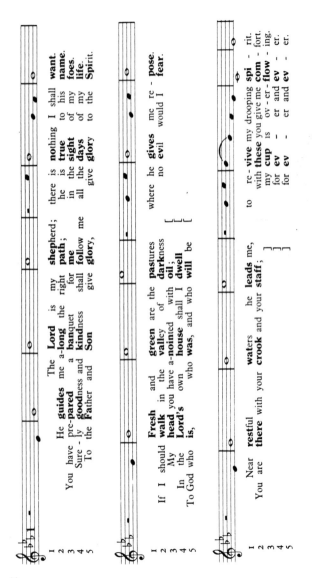

ANTIPHONS

by GELINEAU & MURRAY

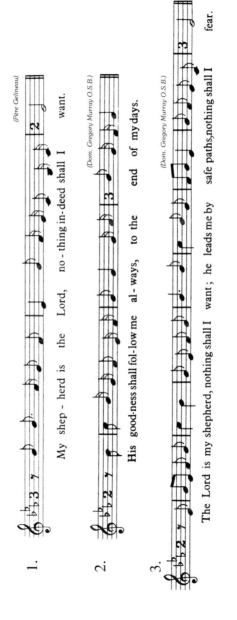

1. My shep - herd is the Lord, no - thing in-deed shall I want. *(Père Gelineau)*

2. His good-ness shall fol-low me al-ways, to the end of my days. *(Dom. Gregory Murray O.S.B.)*

3. The Lord is my shepherd, nothing shall I want; he leads me by safe paths, nothing shall I fear. *(Dom. Gregory Murray O.S.B.)*

Psalm Twenty Three

Don't you love the thought of 'freshness'! We can only appreciate its full meaning when we think of what the opposite of 'fresh' means. But let's not do that right now. Let's instead be with the Good Shepherd, and bask in the joy of these superb words, so brilliantly chosen; fresh, green, pastures, repose, restful waters, revive. Take them into your heart and simply enjoy them in their entirety.

You know, I could spend all day dwelling on these few words, and be as happy as a queen with my Good Shepherd, at the end of the day. They are so rich and full. Each word is luscious! The idea of 'freshness', don't you love it! I do! It conjures up so many wonderful thoughts and images. Fresh air, fresh cool running water, waterfalls, showers, oasis in the desert, clear streams gurgling over the rocks, fresh fish, fresh food, fresh vegetables, cool drinking water, beautiful flowers, blossom, smell of freshly mown grass, smell of clean clothes on the line, freshness of the air after the storm, smell of freshly baked bread, health, cleansing and cleanliness, beauty, waking up after a good rest, fresh complexion, children at play, fun, laughter, joy, spontaneity, enthusiasm, a fresh approach, surprises of a vibrant faith, and so on and on. Thoughts are endless! 'Freshness' speaks so much to me of God!

On the other hand, 'green pastures' conjure up restful scenes of countryside; vast expanses of pasture land; meadows decked with buttercups, cowslips, primroses, bluebells; hedge rows sparkling with wild flowers; cattle peacefully grazing; sheep and lambs frisking about; buds unfolding as the delicate 'new' green of springtime foliage emerges after the winter solemnity, exquisite to behold, with a freshness and 'soft' tender green, never known at any other time of the year in England. But dangerous to the 'dreamer' and 'lover' of God's wonderful world, while driving along

the country lanes! I always marvel at the
beauty of His hand in our countryside.
Let all creation praise Him! Let everything
within me praise Him. Let the whole world
acknowledge His beauty. And as I let the
countryside seep into my being, I think too
of the distant fields of home (Ireland),
where the grass is so green, the countryside
so picturesque and unspoilt, and where the
love on the land is so apparent, the
friendliness and warmth of the green
pastures, the smell of the turf, the welcome
of home! And so I give thanks!

'Green' pastures also suggest space, time
out, friends, walks in the countryside,
holidays, good times, earth and earthiness,
gardening and gardens, seeds and growth,
sleep and rest, peace and contemplation;
prayer, stillness, and silence; renewal and
refreshment, fruitfulness and faithfulness;
even thoughts on the final 'resting place'
before the last journey, Home! In fact, I'm
reminded of all the lovely things, that give
balance and wholeness to a busy life. The
things we do not get enough of these days,
even the song of the birds!

"The story is told of a monk who went out
one exceptionally fine spring morning to

hear the meadow lark sing and when he returned, all his friends had died; three hundred years had gone by.
To go out in the springtime of our spiritual youth, to listen to the voice of the Good Shepherd, is to pass beyond time. It is to experience however fleetingly what Etienne Gilson describes as 'man's supreme bliss', a foretaste of the face to face vision of motionless eternity". *('For You' by Carl Sandburg, quoted in 'He and I', p. 156)*

I want to lead you now to the 'freshness' of the gift of faith and of the promptings of the Holy Spirit, ever fresh, ever new, ever life-giving. "Near restful waters He leads me!" When you think of the amazing 'freshness' of Vatican 2 Council, and the gift it was to the Catholic Church, through our dear Pope John XXIII, (though well on in years) opening up the windows and letting the fresh air of the Holy Spirit into the Church, you can only marvel at the love of the Good Shepherd for His sheep. No doubt, He saw pockets of staleness in the Church at that time and wanted to bring it new life. What could have been and is to some extent, the most extraordinary grace for the renewal of the church, has yet to come to fruition! We're slow to change!

The windows were thrown wide open to God's power and love, leading the way for a new Pentecost, But were we ready enough for it? Has it yet begun? Have we been responsive enough?

"The Council came like an invitation to conversion from God to each one of us, and we stood on its threshold with momentous but no longer meaningful words. And yet, which makes it all the more serious, these are the very words of Jesus Himself." *('In Search of the Beyond', Carlo Carretto, p. 156)*

There certainly is a wonderful awakening among the laity and religious since then, and a deeper understanding of Christian Vocation, Mission, Parish community and Outreach to the poor of the world, perhaps as never before. Likewise, the gift of Charismatic Renewal has brought a 'new' spiritual awakening to so many throughout the world, through the gifts of the Holy Spirit, leading people to a gift of prayer and understanding of sacred scripture and community, never experienced before. Many married couples will tell you how the renewal has changed their lives for the better, and how it has brought them a deeper prayer life and much more happiness together.

"The wind *(Holy Spirit)* blows where it pleases, you hear its sound,
But you cannot tell where it comes from or where it is going
That is how it is, with all those who are born of the Spirit". *(John 3:8)*

I marvel too at the freshness of the Holy Spirit in our lives and at the many 'God' instances, (too many to count) in our daily lives. Nothing happens by chance, but is wrapped up in God's overall plan for our lives, with no such thing as co-incidences! His love alone watching over our every move! " I have plans for you", He says, "plans for peace and not disaster, reserving a future full of hope for you". *(Jeremiah 29:11)*

My wonderful mother used always say 'God knows best, leave it to Him' and now, I can say the same myself from my own experience. The more we have eyes to see, the more we see. The Holy Spirit certainly keeps you 'fresh' in outlook, young in spirit, never knowing what His next surprise will be for you. It is a very exciting time to be alive in the church.

"You give breath, fresh life begins,
You keep renewing the world." *(Psalm 104:30)*

Let us ask the Good Shepherd to keep
renewing the Church, to rejuvenate it, to
restore it to the joy and enthusiasm of the
First Pentecost. Let us beg Him to send His
Holy Spirit again and again. The Catholic
Church is always praying 'Come Holy
Spirit', but if the Spirit took us at our word
and came in the power of Pentecost, we
would die! *(cf. Acts 2)*

Sometimes we get amazing glimpses of
what the Church should and could be,
especially at times like Christmas and
Easter, where the liturgical ceremonies are
out of this world, and other times of
celebration, baptisms and even funerals! To
share the solemnity of our beloved Pope
John Paul II's Funeral and the ceremony of
inauguration of Pope Benedict XVI with the
whole world, was indeed an immense joy,
which gave us a truly ecstatic sense of the
splendour and majesty and unity of the
Church Family, over which The Good
Shepherd reigns. One felt so proud to be
Catholic! Compared to the evil in the
world, with so much bad news showing on
television, this was such a refreshing

contrast. "Fresh and green are the pastures where He gives me repose, near restful waters He leads me to revive my drooping spirit." *(Psalm 23)* There is no doubt that the Church is always refreshing and life giving, when under the influence of the Holy Spirit. Unfortunately the members are not always fully alive to the Spirit of God, and so, can easily get in a rut, forgetting Jesus and his teaching, at times unable to listen to His Gospel. Some don't like fresh air! We must beware of the danger of becoming stagnant! "Go out to the whole world, proclaim the Good News to all creation" is Jesus' command. *(Mark 16:16)*

The Church must be constantly looking outwards to the different needs of the world, always missionary in character and always ready to bring the Good News of Jesus Christ wherever it is needed, otherwise it would be failing the Good Shepherd. Just as it says in our rule of life, 'there is no mission without adoration', so too for the church, there is no church without mission.

'We need to change and become converted; we must effectively build up a Church which will be the Church of the poor, the Church of the Spirit, the charismatic Church... ' *('In Search of the Beyond', Carlo Carretto, p.8)*

We wouldn't know what to do if the Holy Spirit came more powerfully. Vatican 2 was truly an amazing chance for the Church. God is always giving us chances!

Do you remember how we saw the Holy Spirit sweeping the world with Alpha (through the witness and ingenuity of Nicky Gumble and Sandy Millar, two specially chosen shepherds of the flock)? Alpha is an anointed Evangelisation course, which leads people to faith in Jesus Christ, the Good Shepherd. Many are coming to faith and new life in God through this programme.

We see in our day also, in a spectacular way, the power of God at work in many missionaries especially people like the late Mother Teresa and her communities, doing such beautiful work for God, with the poorest of the poor, giving the poor from the streets, a dignity they may never have known, while preparing others for a happy and peaceful death.

The former pop-star Bob Geldof is also a prophetic voice today, in calling the world to

help the poorer countries, leading people in
another way, knowingly or unknowingly, to
serve Jesus Christ, present in His poor.
Through his recent gathering together of
peoples and pop stars from all over the
world, his magnificent 'Live 8' concert in
Hyde Park London raised millions for charity
in Africa. He created a huge awareness of
our shared responsibility to help the poor.
He pleads with the richer governments to
'make poverty history' by cancelling the third
world debt completely, and help to wipe out
poverty.

A wonderful friend of ours, Fr. Gerald Vann,
at the age of seventy four, has just returned
from two months generous service to the
poorest of the poor in Rwanda. He has
never seen such desperate poverty. The
children haven't enough food and their
clothes are rags! Such energy for God!
What a blessing his visit was for them! Does
the Holy Spirit ever stop calling us? You're
never too old to do a new thing for Him.

However, Jesus Himself says: "the poor you
have always with you." *(John 8:12)* so,
perhaps, if Jesus has said this, we will
always have the poor with us. We must
continually fight for them and cry out

against the evil of poverty. To encourage us in our acts of charity, Jesus assures us that: "What you do to Mine, you do to Me. For I was hungry and you gave Me food; I was thirsty and you gave Me drink; I was a stranger and you made Me welcome; naked and you clothed Me; sick or in prison and you went to see Me." *(Matthew 25:35-36,40)* And again He says: "If anyone gives so much as a cup of cold water to one of these little ones because he is a disciple, then I tell you solemnly, he will most certainly not lose his reward." *(Matthew 10:42)* Certainly a good incentive to give generously!

What a privilege to serve Him in His poor! Our poorer brothers and sisters around the world, especially in Africa, are suffering desperately from dire poverty and starvation, disease and deprivation. They are dying at an enormous rate. It is so horrendous. They are indeed our Family who need our help. God's Family, one world! His World!

Pray, pray, pray, change our hearts Lord and make us care more. Make us generous. Everyone present at the Live 8 Concert, must surely have seen the blaze and 'power' of the Holy Spirit at work (as one of our sisters witnessed) as the spirit of goodness, love, joy, togetherness, generosity, fun, music, good will, peace, all reigned supreme, as never before in the great City of London. Those who were present would find it hard to put into words the *power* present on that occasion, but it surely was the creative power of God using us weak human beings. *A gathering like this can only be of God!* Everyone present was greatly moved. In a sense, it was the church in action! We pray Bob Geldof succeeds in his dream.

It just takes one voice to sing a song and one person to make a difference.

"How beautiful on the mountains are the feet of the one who brings Good News, who heralds peace, brings happiness." (Isaiah 52:7)

Sometimes God gives you many happinesses together, and London's next happy experience was the splendour and triumph of being chosen to host the next Olympic Games in 2012. Such an honour! Such Joy! People, when they heard the great news, were even crying with happiness and were so excited they didn't know how to contain their happiness.

Goodness, beauty and rejoicing are
obviously always too much for the evil one
to take so, of course, he has to try to
disrupt the peace and harmony.

Note that he frequently tries to upset families
at times of celebration, especially Christmas
time, and God gets the blame. In fact, I hear
that the seeds of most divorces happen
around Christmas time, true or untrue! How
stupid we can be too, not to see what is going
on! The devil's plan is always only to destroy.
And so, on the day following this triumphant
jubilation in London, we hear of the diabolic
attack on London's Transport System, with
bombs exploding at rush hour in three
underground trains and a bomb on a London
bus on the same day, killing several innocent
people and injuring hundreds more.

Such a barbaric and evil happening, most
certainly was the work of the devil! (In
contrast to what we saw God doing the day
before in London). This evil was the work
of five suicide bombers, who plotted
against the Peace! *(Suicide bombers are
surely one of the greatest evils of our time).*

As people's joy was so quickly turned to
sadness some were saying, "Why didn't

God stop this. He could if he wanted to?"
Yes, He could of course. But remember
that God has given each human being free
will to use for good or ill. He will not
interfere with how we use this gift, which
makes us different from the animals. How
would you like Him interfering with your
decisions? How we live is our choice.
Hence the importance of using our free will
for good not evil. Don't you need to stop
blaming God for the things that go wrong?

God is Good! God is Love! God is
Happiness! God is beauty! The Good
Shepherd spent His whole public life
working for good, conquering the evil of
suffering and sickness, and restoring
people's peace. "Jesus made a tour of the
towns and villages, teaching in their
synagogues, proclaiming the Good News
of the Kingdom and curing all kinds of
diseases and sicknesses. And when He saw
the crowds, He felt sorry for them, because
they were harassed and dejected, like sheep
without a shepherd." Then He said to His
disciples: "The harvest is rich but the
labourers are few, so ask the Lord of the
harvest, to send labourers to His harvest."
(Matthew 9:35-37) The church needs more
good labourers and witnesses to help

spread the Good News of Jesus. Are you one of these labourers? What a scandal if we as Church will not love and care for God's poor! Church is not about respectability and ritual, but about service. 'I give you a new commandment: 'Love one another just as I have loved you',' Jesus said. *(John 15:12)* "To separate our love for God from our love of our fellow man is a fundamental betrayal of the Gospel ideal." *('In search of the Beyond': Carlo Carretto, p.156*

Jesus was the Servant of all. He goes beyond ritual. "The Church that concentrates on its own ritual and is not aware of the suffering and anxiety of people, of the chains that bind them, is a dead church, with nothing more to say about the heart and mind of its Founder." *(Ibid)*

The Church must always be missionary, always like Jesus, its leader. "And there are other sheep I have that are not of this fold and these I have to lead as well. They too will listen to My Voice, and there will be only one flock and one Shepherd." *(John 10:16)* So there is lots of work for the church to do, and much prayer needed. Jesus Himself told us: "I came for the lost sheep of the House of Israel." *(Matthew 15:25)*

From time to time, the Holy Spirit calls us to a great awakening of heart. He gives us special opportunities, always trying to move us on to greater freshness, love and commitment and to wider pastures. The problem is that our response is poor, sometimes slow, and even lazy; our comfort zones might be disturbed and so our response remains weak and half hearted.

The Holy Spirit can see through us and knows we pray only half-heartedly! He sees the depths. Perhaps our prayer needs to become more fervent. We must desire and pray more for growth and for the changes that the Holy Spirit wants. Our faith needs to become more vibrant. "I will give them life", Jesus says in John 14:6. "The world must be brought to know that I love the Father," Jesus added. *(John: 14:31)* Yes! Making the world aware that Jesus came from God the Father and that their love for each other forms the Holy Spirit, is a sacred part of the Church's mission.

Christian Faith is the best gift of all. It is so beautiful and makes everything beautiful and possible. What would we do without it? To what can we compare this wondrous gift? The pearl of great price, the treasure hidden in the field. *(cf. Matthew 13:44)* There would be such emptiness in our lives without it. How can anyone live without believing in God, I wonder. I can't imagine how empty atheists' and agnostics' lives must be. You may gain the whole world but if you don't know a personal God, what emptiness! What poverty! Faith is not just about adhering to revealed truths, it is, in fact, an encounter with the living God, who reveals Himself to the individual, and who for the believer, becomes the light of his pilgrimage. Continually thank God for this priceless gift. Continually pray for others to receive it.

"Your Word is a lamp for my feet, a light on my path." *(Psalm 18:28)*
"Yahweh is my light and my salvation, whom need I fear." *(Psalm 27:1)*
"Anyone who follows Me, will not be walking in the dark, but will have the light of life." *(John 7:12)*

Faith is a journey with the Good Shepherd. "If we live by Faith, we're not boring and stale. *(opposite of fresh!)* Our soul becomes filled with fresh thoughts, fresh tastes, fresh judgements, fresh enthusiasm. Fresh horizons open up before us. The world lives in the darkest night. The man or woman of faith basks in a brilliant splendour of God's radiance! The bright path he or she treads is unseen by men, who seem to be setting off into emptiness, like the fool." *(Charles de Foucauld Letter, 08.07.01)*

So, if you have the gift of faith treasure it. If it is weak, ask the Good Shepherd to strengthen it. If you have no faith, I pray for you, that you may desire it, and receive it humbly. You cannot force it or earn it. You can only respond and receive it when the Holy Spirit gives it to you, touching your innermost being. All is mystery, you know. Faith is a mystery, it cannot be rationalized or achieved through one's own efforts. It is a total Gift of God. People sometimes say to me: "I wish I had your faith." I say: "You could, if you want, just ask God for it." He never refuses the Holy Spirit to those who ask." *(cf. Luke 11:13)* It's bad enough not to have faith, but it must be worse to have had it and then to lose it and worse still to let it die all together.

"A man without faith (God) is, ipso facto,
  a lung without air,
  an eye without light,
  a heart without love." *('In search of the Beyond': Carlo Carretto, p.156)*

If people only knew the joy and beautiful assurance of faith. If only they would take this magnificent Psalm 23 'The Lord Is my Shepherd,' to heart, hug it, and love it, and cherish it and try to live it, their lives would change overnight.

Charles de Foucauld *(the posthumous Founder of the little Brothers and Sisters of Jesus)* lost his faith for twelve years, and during this time, he pleaded with God: "My God, if you exist, help me to know You". God is always finding opportunities for us and He speaks to us 'where we are' if we are listening.

Carlo Carretto writes: "Islam shook me deeply… seeing such faith… seeing people living in the continual presence of God. I came to glimpse something bigger and more real, than worldly occupations." *(Lettres à Henry de Castries)*

It was through seeing the faith of the Jews and Muslims among whom he was called, that he was changed and came towards faith. Interesting to note in the Gospels, that it was a Samaritan leper who returned to give Jesus thanks *(Luke 17:18,19)* and it was a Samaritan in the parable who shared kindness and who proved to be the neighbour to the man who fell among robbers. *(Luke 10:37)* It is the opposite to what we might think.

'Fresh and green are the pastures where He gives me repose', Yes, always! When God wants to work, He creates freshness and hope. He can use anyone, in any situation at any time. Are our minds too tunnel visioned or even closed? Do we block his work by setting limits to God's power? Do we see it is His hand at work? Is our faith too weak? Jesus said of the centurion that He had never seen such faith in Israel. *(Matthew 8:10)*. The Jews might have been expected to have such faith but certainly not a Samaritan!

Charles de Foucauld looked for faith, as one looks for evidence of proofs. He searched for God, he combed the books of pagan philosophers but found nothing but emptiness and disgust…

He writes: "And by Your grace, I chanced on a Christian Book: 'Elévations sur les Mystères by Bossuet, and felt the warmth and beauty… You encouraged me to feel that there I might perhaps find, if not truth,

(I did not believe men could know the truth) at least instruction in the paths of virtue, and inspired me *(still pagan!)* to look for it in Christian Books... In this way, You familiarized me with the mysteries of religion... More and more, You drew me to the truth by the beauty of 'her' soul, and then You lavished Your graces on me."
(Charles de Foucauld: 'Silent Pilgrimage to God', pp. 16-17)

"Near restful waters He leads me to revive my drooping spirit". The journey towards the faith, what a journey! Remember Jesus said "I am the Way" *(John 15:6)*   It's like coming upon an oasis in the desert.

How very clever of God. He never misses an opportunity to draw a soul closer to Him. Because He sees the whole picture, He can so subtly, so cleverly, use every situation for His purposes. If only we could discern His ways and 'catch on' more quickly!

"Why do you doubt, you of little faith?
Am I less great than yesterday?
Could My Love ever fail?
Do I love you for what you are worth?
Or, as always, for your poverty?
Does love seek its own interest?

The Love of a God! Haven't I taken you as
you are: with all that you know of your weak-
nesses? Then why, after so many free gifts,
should you doubt My merciful goodness?
Haven't I told you that justice is for later on?

Close the eyes of this fear that paralyses
you and throw yourself into my arms. I am
the very gentle Shepherd; you know that
I'll give you rest on My heart. What matters
most of all is the fusion of our two wills -
'on earth, as in heaven.' No refusal, then.

Perfect acceptance, not forced, but with
tenderness and from the desire to be then
ever united to me. The more you are in
Me, the smaller you are in yourself and the
greater you are in Me. Come close to your
heaven. Heaven is our oneness – your
mind in My mind. Begin, My child, My very
own." *('He and I', Gabrielle Bossis, p.77)*

Those who seek God find Him, I have no
doubt about that. God is always there.
The ball is always in our court! We are
sometimes so stubborn! How does He
cope with us! The beautiful psalms tell us:
"Make Yahweh your only joy and He will
give you your heart's desire." *(Psalm 37:4)*
Or again we read: "Your love is better than

life itself, my lips will recite your praises, all my life, I will bless You." *(Psalm 63:3)*

"Faith," writes John Powell, S.J., "did not ask too much; it promised too much. It was not that God's Word was too hard to believe, it was rather too good to believe." *('The Christian Vision', John Powell, S.J., p.41)*

How true! Only God can make a person a believer, and all the riches in the world cannot buy the gift of faith, this rich green pasture is God's for the giving and ours for the taking. Make a habit of thanking God frequently for the gift of faith. Ask Him for an increase in it. "If your faith were the size of a mustard seed, you could say to this mountain: 'Move from here to there' and it would move; nothing would be impossible for you," Jesus said. *(Matthew 17:20)*

"They feast on the bounty of Your house; You give them drink from the river of pleasure. With You is the fountain of life." *(Psalm 36:9)*

One day, Charles de Foucauld suddenly saw the light, and he not only believed but gave himself totally to the God he believed in. "As soon as I believed," he writes, "there was a God. I saw that the only course open

to me was to devote myself entirely to Him;
my religious vocation dates from that same
moment as my faith." *(Lettres à Henry de
Castries, 14.08.1901, p.96)*

What grace! Cardinal Newman had a
similar conversion to that of St. Paul and
many others.

> Lead kindly light
> amid th'encircling gloom,
> lead thou me on;
> The night is dark
> and I am far from home,
> lead thou me on.
> Keep thou my feet;
> I do not ask to see
> the distant scene;
> one step enough for me.
>
> I was not ever thus,
> nor prayed that thou
> shouldst lead me on;
> I loved to choose
> and see my path; but now
> lead thou me on.
> I loved the garish day,
> and, spite of fears,
> pride ruled my will;
> remember not past years.

So long Thy power
hath blest me, sure it still
will lead me on
o'er moor and fen,
o'er crag and torrent, till
the night is gone,
and with the morn
those angel faces smile
which I have loved
long since, and lost awhile.
John Henry Newman (1801- 90)

There is nothing like the gift of faith, it transforms your life, and puts you on another plane of living. Jesus said to the apostles that they would be 'in' the world but not 'of' it. *(John 17:14)* Learn from His Word.

As Christians, we do not belong to the world. The world Jesus is talking about is a world of greed, sickness, materialism, paganism, consumerism, Godlessness, and anti-God culture, etc. All the ugly, negative, evil forces... that destroy, divide, disrupt, damage, and cause so much unhappiness. Faith, on the other hand, brings so much security, peace and a lasting deep joy. A living faith is always 'fresh'. It restores life, and gives you benefits beyond your dreams,

with all its loveliness and super abundance.
God gives "full measure, pressed down,
shaken together and running over." This is
God's super abundance, as He can only
give abundantly, leading us to green
pastures, ever fresh!

'Fresh and green pastures where He gives
me repose.' *(Psalm 23)*
Never take the gift of faith for granted.
Thank God often for it, and hold it sacred,
close to your heart. "If you have faith,
everything you ask in prayer, you will
receive," said Jesus. *(Matthew 21:22)*

The Good Shepherd knows his sheep and
He listens to their voice. He longs for this
close relationship with Him that comes
through faith. He wants to give us "the gift
of his love", *(Song of Songs 7:14)* but love
must be received to be ours. Many a parent
wants to love a child who does not want to
receive love! Children sometimes run away
from parent's love, for some reason they
simply can't take it. Such sorrow!

Life and prayer are inseparable. Through
prayer, lifting up our minds and hearts to
God, we realize that everything around us,
has a sacred value in the eyes of God. "You

can do nothing without Me," says Jesus.
(John 15:5)

To enjoy His 'restful waters' pray. He is
always beside you. There are many ways of
praying; simply use a mantra from the
'Lord is my Shepherd' like saying 'My
Shepherd'. Then just keep repeating these
two words several times, till you're still; or
the words: 'fresh and green are the
pastures': or 'He gives me repose' or any
scripture words that appeal to you: Say
them prayerfully and lovingly, and imagine
the Good Shepherd looking after you in
green pastures. This leads to stillness, and
it keeps your mind away from distractions
and from any negative words you may have
heard about yourself!

Don't ever waste precious time on words
other than God's words! Rather take a
passage from Scripture and make it your
own. Read it, identify with one of the
characters in the passage, and imagine the
scene. Pray it through. If you go to
Exposition of the Blessed Sacrament, just
listen to the Lord and let Him speak to your
heart. He has been waiting all day for you
to come. Lovers don't always need to
speak, do they? Tell Him you love Him,

many times. He likes to hear it, as lovers do! 'Enjoy Me. Give yourself a rest from saying prayers,' Jesus says, 'so that you may enjoy My love'. *(Gabrielle Bossis, 'He and I,' p.96)*

'Prayer consists', as St. Teresa tells us, 'not in speaking a lot but in loving a lot'. So, sit with your Good Shepherd 'in' love. If you attend Holy Mass, listen carefully to the readings, there's always something for you, so enriching!

If you can get to daily Mass, that's excellent; you couldn't do better, as the Mass is the greatest expression of prayer to God the Father, the sacrifice of praise. It is offering Him His only beloved Son, Jesus. Make a habit of simply talking to God about everything, especially your worries. If you have a petition, simply ask Him, thank Him, believe it is yours, and it is yours. This is what I do! And it happens! God is so good, especially if you are asking for others' needs. Or again, you could enjoy saying the rosary, or even meditating on one decade.

Use the psalms in your prayer and you will be praying as Jesus prayed as He grew up.

If you're happy, there's a suitable psalm and if you're sad there's a comforting psalm, even if you feel like killing somebody, there's likewise an appropriate psalm. But please don't!! Use these prayers perhaps to put your future in God's hands.

From the psalms, Jesus would have known what was to happen to Him in the future, as many of the psalms foretell about the Messiah. Best I think that we do not know our future, best left in God's hands. Don't you think so? I do! Pray gently and make your prayer time a time of repose. 'Like a weaned child on its mother's breast, so is my soul within me'. *(Psalm 131:2)*

Seeking His will, not your own, in your life, is the best, since that is how the Good Shepherd lived, always seeking His Father's Will. Difficult but worthwhile! "Anyone who does the will of God", Jesus said "that person is my brother, my sister, my mother." *(Mark 3:35)* Jesus also said, "Not everyone who says: 'Lord! Lord! will enter the kingdom of heaven but only those who do the will of My Father." *(Matthew 7:22)*

Try to see that God can bring good out of all circumstances, even the worst; and that

He has your interest at heart. "We know
that by turning everything to their good,
God co-operates with all those who love
Him" *(Romans 8:3)*. Pray 'Our Father' with
confidence. God will not let you down. Try
to simply throw yourself into His arms, and
rest on the gentle Shepherd's breast. Let
your prayer be that *your* will, will fuse with
His, as Jesus always prayed to His Father.
Another type of prayer is the 'Week of
Praise', where, for one whole week in your
life, you simply praise God for everything,
absolutely everything, whether good or bad.
You do nothing but praise.

This has a fantastic effect! Try it! Use your
praise psalms a lot during this week.
Wonderful! You will be amazed at what
praise will do for you. The only words you
must utter during the whole week must be
'praise' words in every area of your life.
Not one single word from your lips, or
thoughts in your heart, must be negative!
God of course, doesn't need your praise.
He just gives a little chuckle and a little
smile, because He can see the value of
praise to our spirits. It is we who gain if we
praise Him.

I remember once when I was a student at

the Guild Hall School of Music in the East
End of London, I very badly needed safer
accomodation particularly as I had to walk
home after rehearsals late at night on my
own. I felt nervous. So I decided that
instead of 'giving out' about this, I would
simply praise God for my problem.

So, I remember sitting on the floor in my
room, with my bible, and I decided I would
pray every praise psalm I could find. It
worked immediately! I made a phone call
that evening to Bishop David Konstant and
through him the very next day, the Lord
found me, the best possible accommodation
in Notting Hill. A quick answer to my
prayer!

"Let everything that lives and breathes,
praise the Lord" *(Psalm 150:6)* which is the
very last verse of the last psalm in the book
of psalms). The original meaning of the
book of Psalms is the book of Praises.

There's so much speed and stress in our
world today, that if we don't train ourselves
to stop and take stock, without letting stress
control our lives, we're in danger of losing
'the music of our own being', and even our
precious gift of health! The result could

have serious consequences for us. We stop
'living'. A great tragedy! Life is not all
about work you know! Jesus' apostles
worked hard for Him, they had opposition
and hardships, but they knew how to opt
out and stay close to the Good Shepherd,
who would lead them to 'Fresh and Green
pastures, beside restful waters', where He
Himself could always give them repose and
refreshment. He used to call them apart to
be by themselves with Him alone.

After He died, they worked solely for Him.
They spread the Good News of His life and
death. They faithfully spread His message.
When they came across opposition and
people trying to stop their good work,
ordering them not to speak aloud in the
name of Jesus, they simply met together
and praised all the louder, so that the room
where they praised shook *(Acts 4:31),* and
they were all filled with the Holy Spirit and
boldness and they ran off again into the
world, to continue shouting out the Good
News that 'Jesus is alive!'

Nothing could stop their love for Him, their
Lord and Saviour. God even worked more
miracles through them after their praise.
With His power at work in them, they were

able to do the impossible. Through their teaching, many people came to know the Lord Jesus, as their Shepherd, and Saviour, and they came to believe in Him. Many were healed.

"So many signs and wonders were worked among the people at the hands of the apostles, that the sick were even taken out into the streets and laid on beds and sleeping-mats in the hope that at least the shadow of Peter might fall across some of them as he went past. People even came crowding in from the towns round about Jerusalem, bringing with them their sick and those tormented by unclean spirits, and all of them were cured." *(Acts 5:12a-16)*

"So remarkable were the miracles worked by God at Paul's hands, that handkerchiefs or aprons which had touched him, were taken to the sick, and they were cured of their illnesses, and the evil spirits came out of them." *(Acts 19:11-12)*

To show that the benevolent Good Shepherd loves his sheep so much, I want to quote for you a short passage from the Gospel, and you will see that Jesus passed on to His disciples His very own giftedness for healing His sheep.

"Having made the crossing, they came to the land of Gennesaret. When the local people recognized Him they spread the news through the whole neighbourhood and took all that were sick to him, begging Him to let them touch the fringe of his cloak. All those who touched it were completely cured." *(Matthew 14:34-36)*

Christians should be different from those who are of the world. Their values and reactions should be different. They should be better able to cope with difficulties, because they should know where to put them – no place other than at the foot of the Cross! The Victory Ground where Jesus conquered sin, death and all evil!

When you feel life's pressures affecting your health, be it ever so slightly, you should stop! You're better off, out of work, living on very little, than be in a job that is detrimental to your health. Peace of mind and good health must be priorities! Take some days off work and recite the psalms.

Pray the 'Lord is my Shepherd'. *(Psalm 23)*. You won't know yourself in one week, if you believe what this psalm says.

Remember you don't belong to the world,
so you can't fit into this pressurised world,
so don't even try! There is much evil
around today especially in this field of work.

To be a Christian is to know that the Lord is
your Shepherd and that there are always
green pastures available through your faith
in Him. I pray the Good Shepherd will
stretch out His crook to capture you, so
that you will know and experience the
superabundance of His grace, not only
sometimes but daily. May He always lead
you to 'restful waters to revive your
drooping spirit'. *(Psalm 23)*

I would like to finish these thoughts with
Charles de Foucauld's amazing prayer of
abandonment. *(Difficult to say and mean fully!)*

> "My Father
> I abandon myself to You.
> Do with me as You will:
> Whatever You may do with me
> I thank You:
> I am prepared for anything:
> I accept everything.
> Provided your will is fulfilled in me
> And in all creatures,
> I ask for nothing more.

My God,
I place my soul in Your hands.
I give it to you My God
With all the love of my heart
Because I love You.
And for me it is a necessity of love,
this gift of myself;
This placing of myself in Your hands
Without reserve;
In boundless confidence
Because You are
My Father."

*(Père Charles de Foucauld, 'Silent
Pilgrimage to God'. pp. 16-17)*

And by the way, did you know that God is everlasting and that His freshness is all pervasive!

Psalm Twenty Three

CHAPTER THREE

He guides me along
the right path
He is true to his Name.

(Psalm 23:3)

© *Watercolour, Terry Harrison*

THE ONLY WAY!

85

THE ONLY WAY !

The God of love My Shepherd is
And He that doth me feed
While He is mine and I am His,
What can I want or need?

He leads me to the tender grass,
Where I both feed and rest;
Then to the streams that gently pass;
In both I have the best.

Or if I stray, He doth convert
And bring my mind in frame;
And all this not for my desert,
But for His holy name.

Yea, in death's shady dark abode,
Well may I walk not fear;
For Thou art with me and Thy rod
To guide, Thy staff to bear.

Surely Thy sweet and wondrous love
Shall measure all my days;
And, as it never shall remove,
So neither shall my praise.

George Herbert (1593-1633)

PSALM TWENTY THREE

This verse brings music to my ears, each word pregnant with the fullness of grace. When you have a reliable guide, all is assured if you decide to follow. You can peacefully trust and have no fear of the unknown, even if you have to travel over rough terrain and through a difficult route. Ramblers know!

This verse conjures up for me, the feeling of warm trust: with the Good Shepherd as Guide, there is a sense of total trust. He alone is omniscient, and consequently He knows every detail of the way, every nook and cranny and He alone can sort out every obstacle. He has trod the way already, and He has given His life for His sheep, a way He may not have liked to go, but, in obedience to his Father He freely and totally accepted the Way because he did not want to lose even one of these sheep! There was a high cost to pay for them, for even a single one on its own, and He paid it in full with his life. Can you imagine it? It was a way that brought Him much suffering but total victory over His attacker. The enemy is now defeated but he is such a liar. 'He was a murderer from the start. He was never grounded in the truth; there is no truth in him at all. When he lies, he is drawing on his own store because he is a liar and the father of lies.' *(John 8:44).* He keeps deceiving people regarding the victory!

Jesus, the Good Shepherd died once, He is not dead any more, He conquered death on the Cross. "Christ Himself, innocent though He was, had died once for sin, died for the guilty, to lead us to God." *(1 Peter 3:18-19)* He is very much alive and it is such a comfort to know this all the time. Do you think about it much? It really is thrilling to know this truth, that Jesus is alive today. He still guides His Flock! He died willingly to rescue us from the evil one. "I lay down My Life of My own free will," Jesus said. *(John 10:18)*

How, therefore, can we ever doubt Him, whom we know and love? He who can never let us down; He who will only ever lead us to what is good, even best for us. It may not seem that way to us. Sometimes He may hide Himself from us to test our love for Him. We may sometimes wonder about the route He takes us on, we may even feel we can't make it. But with Him, as the Good Shepherd, guiding us along, we know that "nothing can come between us and God's love for us, made perfect in Christ Jesus." *(Romans 8:35)* You must always seek His guidance, and though the surface may get ruffled and the route seem hard and tedious, believe deep in your heart, He will bring you through. Though the way appears long, and you think you'll never get there, keep going. What is it compared to eternity?

Life is very short. 'Man lasts no longer than grass, no longer than a wild flower he lives, one gust of wind and he is gone, never to be seen there again.' *(Psalm 103:15-16)* His way has to be the surest way for us, even if we are sometimes tempted to doubt. Maybe, too, we're on His way but we're seeking Him 'in the wrong way', looking for the wrong thing. The Good Shepherd knows best!

"On my bed at night, I sought Him
whom my heart loves.
I sought but did not find Him.
So I will rise and go through the City;
in the streets and the squares,
I will seek Him whom my heart loves.
I sought but did not find Him.
The watchmen came upon me
on their rounds of the City:
'Have you seen Him whom my heart
loves?'
Scarcely had I passed them
than I found Him whom my heart loves."
  (Song of Songs 3:1-4)

In St. John's Gospel, Jesus tells us that He
Himself is the Way, "I am the Way." (John
14:6) and that if we follow His Way, we will
not be walking in the dark. Jesus calls
Himself "The Light of the world." (John 9:5)
There is no way we could travel without the
light, so not only is Jesus the Light and the
Way, but He is also the Food, the Rest, the
Everything as well on the way. He calls
Himself the 'Light of the World' not the
Light of the Jews, or any élite group. He is
the Light of everyone, for everyone, no
favourites, no top nobs here! Where He is,
there is light, and it can only be in His light,
that we see Light. (cf. Psalm 36:9) He is the

Good Shepherd and Guide of all.
King George VI, in his 1939 Christmas
broadcast to the nation, included this
delightful quotation:
"I said to the man who stood at the Gate of
the Year: 'Give me a light that I might tred
safely into the unknown.'
And he replied: 'Go out into the darkness
and put your hand into the Hand of God.
That shall be to you better than a light and
surer than a known way!'"
*(Introduction to 'The Desert' by Louise M. Haskins,
US Writer, 1875-1957)*

There is no other light on the way, and if
there is, it can only be put there by thieves,
as Jesus says, "The thief comes only to
steal." *(John 10:10)*

Can you imagine being blind, not having
light, not being able to appreciate the light?
Imagine the joy of being healed of blindness
by Jesus. "He was sent to give new sight to
the blind." *(Luke 4:18)* Not only is there
physical blindness but there is a worse form
of blindness, called spiritual blindness. Stay
with Jesus' light ! He alone lights up our
way. Beware of thieves 'en route'. Thank
Him for being the light.
The blind man of Jericho cried out: "Jesus,

Son of David, have pity on me! Jesus
stopped and ordered them to bring the man
to Him, and when he came up, asked him,
'What do you want Me to do for you?'
'Sir,' he replied, 'Let me see again.' Jesus
said to him, 'Receive your sight. Your faith
has saved you,' and instantly his sight
returned and he followed Him praising
God, and all the people who saw it gave
praise to God for what had happened."
(Luke 8:34)

"The night is over," St. John says, "and the
'real' light is shining. Anyone who claims
to be in the light but hates his brother is still
in the dark. Anyone who loves his brother
is in the light." *(1 John 2:8-10)*

"Arise, shine out, for your Light has come.
The glory of Yahweh is rising on you,
though night still covers the earth and
darkness the peoples. Above you Yahweh
now rises and above you his glory appears.
The nations come to your light and kings to
your dawning brightness. Lift up your eyes
and look around: all are assembling coming
towards you, your sons from far away and
your daughters being tenderly carried. At
the sight you will grow radiant, your heart
throbbing and full." *(Isaiah 60:1-5)*

The Only Way !

The 'right' path is the very way Jesus
Himself has trod, the path of love and not
without suffering! When we take the wrong
path, (or step out of love) it takes much
longer and we suffer as a result!
Sometimes there has to be a complete
turnabout: we may get hurt, fall, get stuck in
the brambles, or be wounded, attacked, get
totally lost, even get angry at ourselves and
others for being so stupid, for not listening to
the guide, for thinking we know best, and we
may find it hard to get back on track again.
We may even get angry at God!

Sometimes we stubbornly want to stay where
we are, we can't be bothered with the effort it
takes. The path may even be rugged and
mountainous, with many hardships but rather
than admit we're lost, we'll try a little longer
to keep going on the wrong path, not
recognizing we may need help!

The Good Shepherd is always at hand to
help. He certainly knows best what each
sheep needs, and no one knows better than
He. He is so patient. He never deserts His
sheep, (even if they are stupid and can only
blame themselves). He is constantly vigilant
to keep His sheep safe. Although He does
have some obstinate ones!!

"I shall look for the lost one, bring back the stray, bandage the wounded, and make the weak strong. I shall watch over the healthy. I shall be a true Shepherd to them." *(Ezekiel 34:15-16)*

"I have mapped out a path for you alone. Promise Me again to follow it as the one you cherish the most, since I have planned it for you and because coming from Me, it brings you to Me. This is the beautiful highway – the direct route.
Each one has their own path but few follow it. Many invent paths according to their own whims, paths beset with danger and loss. Simplify your pilgrimage to follow My will alone, so as to be sure of fulfilling it faithfully, even to the very smallest details. Fidelity places more value on small opportunities than on big ones. These are the little love-tokens, like the small coins that add up to a fortune. Since you have recognized the road I have marked out for you, don't turn aside from it." *('He and I', Gabrielle Bossis, p.232-3)*

The 'right' path is certainly shown by the Good Shepherd, and as for the love He has shown His sheep, no one could equal it. When the rich young man asked Jesus what He would have to do to gain Eternal Life

(obviously he wanted something more than he already had), Jesus asked him what it said in the law and he replied: "Keep the commandments." The rich young man knew them by heart and was able to recite them for Jesus. "You must not steal, you must not kill, you must not commit adultery, you must not bear false witness against your neighbour, honour your father and your mother, and love your neighbour as yourself. But I've done all this since my youth," the rich young man said.
(Mark 10:17-22)

Then Jesus encouraged him to do a bit more. He's always asking more of us, always offering opportunity for greater commitment, as He waits patiently for our response. He longs for a deeper relationship with us. Are we willing? It's possible for us to live a 'nominal' Christian life and not let it go further: to feel quite content with how life is and not to bother too much about faith. The rich young man couldn't take on board what Jesus was offering. Perhaps his love wasn't strong enough.

The paradox is that it's in giving that we receive, in dying to ourselves we live, in giving love we receive love, in becoming poor we become rich. The rich young man seemed to have been hindered by his love for material possessions, to which he was attached, and so he could not take the next step to greater love. The choice was his and Jesus did not force him. For safety, he could only stay where he was, on the first rung of the ladder of commitment. Jesus was asking more, but gave him his entire freedom.

There's a letting go, for all of us, if we're going to take the Good Shepherd seriously and move on, to a deeper relationship and friendship with Him. Is He asking this of you? He's longing for it. Do you feel this prompting of the Holy Spirit within you? Listen, let your heart keep seeking!

He not only wants to be our guide, but He wants to be our 'best' friend as well. In the Old Testament, the Israelites saw the Shepherd more as a guide. Jesus has transformed the image of the Shepherd by His coming, showing very cleverly that the relationship of Shepherd to sheep is very personal and He wants a relationship of greater intimacy and friendship. The Good Shepherd, calls Himself: 'I am the Good

Shepherd.' *(John 10:14))* He loves each one of His sheep, each is very special to Him, known to Him personally and loved. He knows each one's potential too!

I'm interested here in the word 'good' and in Jesus adding the word 'good' to Shepherd in His dialogue with the rich aristocrat, who put a question to Him: 'Good Master, what have I to do to inherit eternal life?' Jesus said to him: "Why do you call me good? No one is good but God *alone." (Luke 18:18-19)* It is as if Jesus is using this little dialogue to tell us that only God is good, so instead of being the Shepherd, as God was referred to in the Old Testament, He is telling us that He is that same 'God' Shepherd. The 'God' Shepherd is really 'The Good' Shepherd thus qualifying His title rather specially for our comfort. For Jesus said: "Only 'God' is Good."

Then a lawyer to disconcert Him, questioned Him. "Master," he said, "which is the greatest commandment of the law?" Jesus answered "You must love the Lord your God with all your heart, with all your soul, with all your mind, with all your strength. This is the first commandment.

The second resembles this: You must love your neighbour as yourself. On these two commandments hang the whole law and the prophets also." *(Matthew 22: 37- 40)*

So, what is Jesus saying about the 'right' path? Put God first, single-mindedness in His service, desire to please Him, keep His commandments but love your neighbour by becoming a neighbour, and all the rest will follow. In fact He says 'love your neighbour as you love yourself.' This sounds easy and simple but He knows as did the rich young man, how hard it could be. Love God first, then love others 'as' you love yourself.

There is no difference between the way we should love ourselves and the way we should love others. So we have a duty to love others and to love ourselves. In practice, if we follow these guidelines, the result will be beneficial to us. We'll find it easier to love and to receive love. It's in giving that we receive and loving our neighbour won't be such a chore! We would surely experience greater harmony.

"Who is my neighbour?" asked the lawyer. We too get puzzled sometimes as to who is my neighbour? Well, Jesus surprises

everyone with His answer. He was so wise
in his teaching, and used many clever
stories and images from everyday life to
teach people.

In the parable of the Good Samaritan, the
first one we would have expected to have
been the best neighbour failed the test.
The second chap was just as bad, he didn't
make it either.
The third was the outcast, the Samaritan,
the most unlikely one. It was he who
proved to be the neighbour, the one who
loved, the one who showed mercy. Yes,
par excellence, he was the true neighbour!

"How can you love God whom you cannot
see, if you do not love your brother whom
you do see?" St. John asks. *(1 John 4:20)*
Isn't it the same situation in families
sometimes? A family member can actually be
the one who falls victim to unfortunate
circumstances, may be through their own
fault, like the man who fell among robbers,
and they may be the first and nearest person
that needs 'us' to be a neighbour to them.
Often outsiders are better neighbours than
the family, I hear it said, thus causing regret,
sadness and even hurt. Families will do for
others, what they will not do for their very

own! They have care, thought, generosity, for outsiders, but not for their immediate family. They will share with outsiders all sorts of things, but not with their immediate family. They will do things for outsiders but not for their own. There is need for conversion in this area and for a greater love and may be better neighbourliness. Is this your experience?

The challenge is always to love more, and it seems to be the most difficult to love when it's closer to home! What pains love is indifference, being ignored, apathy, and thoughtlessness. The only 'right' path, is the path of love. Always to do the kindest thing! Always to show mercy, always to be a neighbour. Nothing, and no one, can fault kindness. We're winners when we're kind. "Be kind, be kind, be kind, and you will be saints," St. John used to say to his disciples in his later years. We shall be judged on love alone. "Love is the one thing that cannot hurt your neighbour; that is why it is the answer to every one of the commandments." *(Romans 13:10)*

Faith and hope will pass away but only love will remain. It is the greatest. The people we want to remember most in life are those who really love us and show us kindness. I hear of so much hurts in families because people are not kind to each other. It makes me so sad.

Looking back over my own school days, I'm reminded of one very special teacher we had, the only teacher in fact who stands out in my mind. She was a young woman (who later became a Presentation nun), who had a dreadful time from the head mistress who showed her up in front of us young ones in class, because she couldn't get the register right! We really loved this little teacher who cared so much for the poorer children in the class, that I shall never forget her.

The head nun was hard on these poor children, who were sometimes late for school, and this teacher stuck up for them. Part of it, I think was, that their parents couldn't pay for certain items, like school books, and couldn't get the children to school on time. I vividly remember the scenes in the classroom when the headmistress verbally attacked this young teacher in front of us. I can still see her tears for these children. Her gentle heart taught us compassion, mercy and love. No wonder we loved her. Everyone is moved by compassion unless they have 'stone' hearts! Now the Good Shepherd wants a word with

us today. He wants to share some very
special words with us and He would love us to
just sit and rest with Him awhile.

He says: *"As the Father has loved Me,
so I have loved you. Remain in My
love. If you keep My commandments
you will remain in My love, just as I
have kept My Father's commandments and remain in His love. I have
told you this, so that My own joy may
be in you and your joy be complete.
This is My commandment: love one
another, as I have loved you.*

*A man can have no greater love than
to lay down his life for his friends.
You are My friends, if you do what I
command you. I shall not call you
servants any more, because a servant
does not know his master's business: I
call you friends, because I have made
known to you everything I have learnt
from My Father. You did not choose
Me. No, I chose You: and I have
commissioned you to go out and to
bear fruit, fruit that will last and then
the Father will give you anything you
ask Him in My name. What I
command you is to love one another."*
(John 15:9-17)

We shall be judged on *love alone*, not on intelligence, wealth, ability or high position. Jesus tells us, that even if we give as little as a cup of cold water *in His name*, it will not go without its reward. He gave us a 'new' commandment to 'love one another' as He has loved us. How difficult to emulate when you see the sort of love He showed us and still does! 'Impossible', you say and so it is; but with Him, the impossible is possible, so we must struggle on with our 'puny' efforts to love our neighbour and to 'be' a neighbour. "Anyone who loves his brother is living in the light." *(1 John 2:10)* Keeping His commandments without love is useless and keeping the 'letter of the law' without love is fruitless. The message is: 'Go and be a neighbour, be the good Samaritan, love intensely.

According to the Good Shepherd's teaching, any person of any nationality is my neighbour, so my love and help should be as wide as God's Love, no limits! The neighbour in the Good Samaritan parable, was not the one who fell among thieves (as the children usually think). No, it was the one who helped and showed mercy, kindness and generosity. Also, my neighbour is the person who may or may

not, have made a mess of life, who may
even have brought all their troubles on
themselves. *(Like the very stupid man in the
parable, who risked a dangerous road,
unprepared).*

Common sense would have told him that he
should not have gone on this very
treacherous road from Jerusalem to Jericho
alone and unprotected. It was an utterly
crazy thing to do. It would have been a
foregone conclusion that he would be
attacked, robbed of his goods and even
killed by bandits! Everyone knew how
dangerous this road was.

We might say he was naive in the extreme
and very unwise. We might say, too, he
deserved what he got! But Jesus is
expecting us to love him, to be a neighbour
to him. He is recommending the kindness,
compassion and generosity shown to him
by the Samaritan stranger. This seems to
be what Jesus is teaching us – kindness
with non-judgemental attitudes, i.e. loving
respect. Do your best to get him out of the
mess, Jesus is saying, and if you haven't the
total where withal to do it now, at least
start and do something. Do what you can!
'Be compassionate,' Jesus tells us, 'as My

Father is compassionate.' *(Luke 6:36)*
What a standard! Do you know anyone
who lives up to this standard? I only know
one! We're not to judge people. We can
judge the situation but not the person! Very
hard isn't it ? But that is the Good
Shepherd's standard for us. I think I will
have to start immediately as I have failed so
often. How about you? Are you well up on
this ladder of kindness and compassion?

Parents sometimes are really challenged to
do the best for their children, especially if
the latter have made a mess of their lives,
and want their parents to bale them out!!
They find it so hard to love them, as they
do not approve of how they are living and
are so sad, too, when the children seem to
neglect God, when they wander off, get in
such a mess, won't go to Church, and act
unwisely.

I always advise parents: Never stop loving
your children. Never close the door on
them: leave the door at least slightly open
and so give them space to come back. In
fact what a child needs most at any age, is
a parent's love. If only every parent
understood the strength of this bond. It is
often my prayer for parents.

The message of what to do for them is very clear. Never stop loving them! Do what you can for them and in the end only Love wins.

Children may similarly be challenged by their parents, who have perhaps also made a mess of their lives. The children find it hard to love and forgive their parents. They never want to stop loving their parents and find loads of excuses for their behaviour always giving them the benefit of the doubt. They always hope for things to be better. There is so much love in children's hearts for parents. I find it so all the time. Such compassion!

Back to the Good Samaritan. He went off about his business and wisely enlisted the help of the innkeeper. Note, he still continued on his journey but cared enough to say to himself: "I'll do it, if this is the only thing I can do right now, and later on, on my way back, I'll give some more help if necessary."

There's another lesson in the story for us – the lovely trust of the innkeeper. May be he already knew the good nature of this Samaritan; may be he was a frequent visitor and wasn't surprised at his kindness. It

could be he didn't know him at all, which
makes the trust doubly poignant.
Whichever way, he was a kind of good
neighbour, too.

Perhaps this Good Samaritan wasn't
hindered by 'conditioning and judgemental
attitudes' to things and situations as we
sometimes are. No one knows all the
circumstances of any situation. To be a
good neighbour, you don't need to know
everything. Abraham once entertained
three strangers (angels) without knowing it,
(Genesis 8 1-15) and Jesus Himself reminds us
that what we do to the least of His brothers,
we do to Him! "What you do to Mine you
do to Me." *(Matthew 25:40)*
Let's try and get on with it and do our best
for Him, so as to be a good neighbour!

The priest, the 'holy' one, was afraid to
become 'unclean', in which case he
was prohibited from celebrating the liturgy
for a week. *(cf. Leviticus 22:4-7)* The Levite
was afraid to get involved and played safe.
Our judgements or maybe our
misjudgements of situations, may hinder us
from being loving 'neighbours' and from
doing the 'right' thing, the most loving
thing.

This sometimes leaves us with unfortunate regrets. I say to people sometimes, I'd rather have flowers now, not when I'm dead!! When you see flowers at funerals sometimes from people who hardly bid each other the light of day, (and yet they can 'squander' money on flowers at the graveside), it seems to me to be ridiculous. Don't wait till people are dead to love them! Act this very moment!. Start today being a good neighbour. The Master requires it! *Only love wins!*

Compassion to be 'real', must be seen in deeds. Jesus told the lawyer to "Go and do the same yourself!" To learn from a Samaritan! He couldn't have liked that at all. He may have thought he was the 'goodie', and had nothing to learn from his sort. God's Love was obviously in the Samaritan's heart, even though he would have been classed as a heretic! We will be judged on love, not by our creed, but by the life we live, the love we show, no matter how we learn. All that matters is that we learn!

"Be ambitious for the higher gifts. And I am going to show you a way that is better than any of them.

*If I have all the eloquence of men or
of angels, but speak without love, I
am simply a gong booming or a
cymbal clashing.
If I have the gift of prophecy, understanding all the mysteries there are,
and knowing everything,
and if I have faith in all its fullness,
to move mountains, but without love,
then I am nothing at all.
If I give away all that I possess, piece
by piece,
and if I even let them take my body
to burn it,
but am without love, it will do me no
good whatever.*

Love **is always patient and kind;
it is never jealous.**

Love **is never boastful or
conceited,**

**It is never rude or selfish;
It does not take offence, and is
not resentful.**

Love **takes no pleasure in other
people's sins,**

**but delights in the truth;
It is always ready to excuse, to
trust, to hope,
and to endure whatever comes.**

Love does not come to an end.

(1 Corinthians: 13:1-8,12)

"Each one of us can only live a fragment of Christ's life at one time, perhaps one moment of it, or one incident or one experience. But, through our communion with one another in Him, through our oneness with one another, because of His one life in us all, we make up what is wanting in one another and are whole, and in us all, as One Body, His whole life is lived". *(Caryll Houselander, 'The Reed of God', p. 104)*

Though our good deeds may be minuscule and our neighbourliness less than perfect, let us start to listen to the Good Shepherd, and put love wherever we can, be a neighbour as often as we can, and endeavour to stay on His path, which will always lead to abundant blessings.

"Planted in the house of the Lord they will flourish in the courts of our God, still bearing fruit when they are old, still full of sap, still green, to proclaim that the Lord is just. In Him, my rock, there is no wrong." *(Psalm 91)*

"He is true to His name." *(Psalm 23)*
Not only is Jesus the Good Shepherd, true to His Name, He is Truth itself. Jesus revealed the Holy Spirit to us as the Spirit of Truth, whose great work is to bring

God's truth to us. We call it revelation, and no passage in the New Testament shows us what we might call the principles of revelation, better than St. John.

"A man can have no greater love than to lay down his life for his friends. You are My friends, if you do what I command you ." and so on... *(John 16:12-15)*

Revelation is a continual opening out of the meaning of Jesus. It comes to us not from books or creed, but from the living person of Jesus Himself. The nearer we live to Him, the Good Shepherd, the better we will know Him, and the more we will be able to walk in His way. The more we become like Him, the more He will be able to tell us, because we will become more and more receptive to Him, and hear His voice more quickly.

To enjoy His revelation, we must accept Him as Lord and Master.

"If we live by the truth and in love, we shall grow in all ways into Christ, who is the Head." *(Ephesians 4:15)*

I'd like to share with you a miracle prayer, if you wish, where you can make Jesus the Lord of your life, and you will never be able

to count the blessings, if you do.   This
prayer has a dramatic effect on peoples'
lives. Why not consider it, if you have not
already used it. It certainly does change
peoples' lives. It changed mine dramatically
in 1975 and I haven't looked back since! It
will help you to make Jesus Lord of your
life. What better could you do? He longs
for this moment.

Commitment Prayer:

'Lord Jesus Christ, I want to belong to you
from now on.
I want to be freed from the dominion of
darkness and all satan's evil works.
I want to enter into your Kingdom and be
part of your people.
I will turn away from all wrong doing, and I
will avoid everything that leads me to
wrongdoing.
I ask you to forgive me all the sins I have
committed. I forgive everyone who has
ever hurt me.
I offer my life to you and I promise to obey
you as my Lord. I ask you to baptize me in
your Holy Spirit.
I ask you to give me the gift of tongues, the
gift of joy, the gift of praise, the gift of
gratitude, the gift of peace, Amen.
(Taken from the pamphlet 'New Life in the Spirit')

So, to return again to psalm 23. "He guides me along the right path, He is true to His Name." The name, Jesus, was given by the Angel to His Mother Mary, at His conception:
"You must name Him, 'Jesus'." *(Luke 1:32)*

This name, is the name above all other names. The only name whereby we can be saved. Let us say it reverently now. "For of all the names in the world given to men, this is the only one, by which we can be saved." *(Acts 4:12)* It is the only name that has power, and the only name that has healing. *(Acts 3:6)*

It was faith in the Name of Jesus that founded the Church. Say the name with love. Say it often. Use it as a mantra. Use it as you go to sleep, let it lull you to sleep if you can't sleep. Use it to protect yourself in danger, in times of decision and anxiety, in times of fear and hopelessness, to bring comfort in sadness and bereavement. Let it be your joy, let it remind you that God is with you. *(cf. Acts 18:10)* Anoint yourself with it. Say His name, 'Jesus', often.
"I keep Yahweh before me always, for with Him at my right hand, nothing can shake me." *(Psalm 16:8)*

And so I leave you with these comforting
though challenging words of our Good
Shepherd:
"He guides me along the right path, He is
true to His name." *(Psalm 23)*

The Good Shepherd is the Guide who will
never falter. He will never lead you astray.
When we allow His Word to touch us, it will
lead us to intimate life with Him.
"Do your best," says the Good Shepherd,
"I will do the rest. I have to wait upon you,
it's not the other way round, remember."
And so the Good Shepherd guides us along
the 'right' path, true to His name.

And by the way, did you know that the Good Shepherd is omnipresent, and He pursues you always!

If you go to the ends of the earth or the furthest limits of the sea or the sky or the moon, He will still be there.

You will never walk alone!

PSALM TWENTY THREE

CHAPTER FOUR

**You are there with
Your crook and Your staff.
With these You give me comfort.**

(Psalm 23:4)

He cares for me!

The Lord is my Shepherd;
I have everything I need.
He lets me rest in green meadows;
He leads me beside peaceful streams.
He renews my strength.
He guides me along right paths,
bringing honour to His Name.

Even when I walk
through the dark valley of death,
I will not be afraid,
for You are close beside me.
Your rod and staff
protect and comfort me.

You prepare a feast for me
In the presence of my enemies.
You welcome me as a guest,
anointing my head with oil.
My cup overflows with blessings.

Surely goodness
and unfailing love
will pursue me
all the days of my life,
And I will live in the house
of the Lord, forever.

(New Bible, Tyndale)

Psalm Twenty Three

Jesus, our Good Shepherd, wants His sheep to be at peace. He is aware that life is not always safe and easy, and should the sheep go through the valley of darkness, they need not be afraid, for He is there beside them with His crook and His staff, to rescue them. The Good Shepherd is prepared for the enemy, knowing he will attack the sheep. The sheep hear their Master's voice and know it. They don't listen to other voices. "The sheep take no notice of them," Jesus tells us. *(John 10:8)*

In the time of Jesus, shepherds in the Holy Land used their staff as a weapon to defend themselves and their flock, against marauding beasts and robbers. The shepherd had his

rod or crook, with which he used to catch
and pull back any sheep that tried to stray
away. At the end of the day, when the sheep
went into the fold, the shepherd held his rod
low down across the entrance; every sheep
had to pass under it. *(Ezekiel 20: 37)*. In this
way the shepherd could check the sheep, to
see if any had received injury that day.

The image of Jesus as the Shepherd, shows
us a very precious relationship of shepherd
to sheep. The Good Shepherd's sheep are
well cared for. He calls them by name. He
wants the best for each one. He wants
security and peace and healing for them.
"Peace I bequeath to you, My own peace I
give to you, a peace the world cannot give,
this is My gift to you. Do not let your
hearts be troubled or afraid." *(John 14: 27)*

I would like to share with you some
thoughts on inner healing, especially if
your hearts are troubled right now. This is
the healing of our deepest being; body,
mind, and spirit, which includes healing of
hurt memories and dreams as well. It is the
Holy Spirit's beautiful gift to the Church
today, to help restore a person. The Good
Shepherd wants our wholeness. The Holy
Spirit has shown us a wonderful way, to

have our hurts healed and our lives 'mended'. God can heal us even in our dreams. Our dreams can be healing, too.

We can miss opportunities for 'personal' growth, and remain stunted in the life Jesus came to bring us. "I have come," says Jesus, "that they may have life and have it abundantly." *(John 10:10)* Jesus meant these words when He said them. He wants us to have a fuller life. He wants us to experience new life in Him. So many struggle with difficulties that sap all their energy and they do not experience this life Jesus wants to give them. Their energies are all used up in 'survival'!

I have good news for you. Through letting God's Word dwell in you, applying it to your daily life, you can become a 'new' person, and you will begin to live.
More good news is that we 'can' change. We can experience a fullness of life never known before. I know. It happened to me 1975. I came alive in Him, with a new joy, a love for His word previously unknown, a lightness in my spirit, an awareness of His living Presence and a trust beyond all understanding. "Lord do not disappoint me in my trust" *(Psalm 25:1)*

He never will let us down. I've learnt we
need to go nowhere else, except to the
Good Shepherd, who keeps a vigilant watch
over all His sheep, so beautifully. It's all so
simple and possible with Jesus. It will
happen for you, by you yourself taking the
time to apply God's Word to your life and
circumstances, and believing the truth of the
Word. In fact, you yourself are the 'Key'
person in your healing and new life. The
result could be phenomenal. You have to
decide to co-operate with God's Word, by
truly believing it. I have seen so many lives
restored through the power of God's living
Word applied to people's lives. Why not
give this method a try? It works!

For myself, I used to think I was very alive,
having a fairly full happy life. Since I've
discovered Inner Healing, looking back over
my life, I now know for sure, that there is a
much fuller, fresh, joy-filled life, open to
anyone who cares to go for it. Other
people who have experienced inner healing
in this way will agree with me. I don't know
anything like it. Like the best tonic!

So what am I talking about in this chapter?
I'm talking about something possible. I'm
talking about change. I'm talking about a

way of living that many people (living lives of quiet desperation) would long for, if they knew how to get it. I'm talking about a life of lived faith, which produces joy, peace, forgiveness, and happiness, in spite of difficulties and setbacks. I'm talking about a life on earth, where Jesus is truly alive for you. I'm talking about a living faith in the living Lord Jesus. I'm talking about a life of prayer, not a life of saying 'set' prayers, but a life of contemplation and communion with the living God, which takes you above the humdrum events of any day, puts you on another plane of living, with a 'secret' that is all yours and that nothing can touch. You can still enjoy your rosaries etc., but try to develop this contemplative approach.
"If anyone loves Me, he will keep My word, and My Father will love Him, and we shall come to him and make our abode with him." *(John 14:23)*

Take Jesus at His word! He, the Good Shepherd, is living with you no matter where you turn. He is living in you. Let Him become more and more a conscious part of your daily life. Abide in His living Word to you daily. Don't waste your time 'sleep walking'. Wake up to the living Word of God. It is dynamite! Always alive and active!

As you do this, you can: "Unload all your
worries onto Him, for He is looking after
you". *(1 Peter 5:8)* Let the words of Psalm
23, especially, live in you, take root in you.
Read these words often during any one day,
with the Good Shepherd Himself,
particularly if you are going through a
rough patch and life is difficult. Focus away
from yourself and towards the Good
Shepherd. This takes practice sometimes!
You would be surprised at the peace these
words will bring to you. They will help to
restore balance and equilibrium to your
spirit. They will give your life a new
simplicity, a new umph!

Should you decide to take the way of Inner
Healing, you will never be sorry. You will
have found a way and you will be a Winner!
It's like discovering a Stradivarius violin in
your cupboard, never knowing you had it
there, and being able to play it, producing
the most exquisite music from it, after years
of being hidden away. Now your age really
doesn't matter at all with the Lord. Never
too young, never too old, the Lord has all in
hand for you! Just begin today.

I'm glad the Holy Spirit has shown us this
lovely way, shown us how to pray, not only

for ourselves, but also with others and for them for healing, giving us all the gifts we need, gifts beyond our comprehension. "All our qualifications come from God." *(2 Corinthians 3:5)* It is all God's work and how privileged we are, to be chosen to work with Him in this life-giving, miraculous way. We see lives made whole through prayer. We witness spiritual, psychological, emotional, and even physical healing sometimes.

Inner Healing works like this. It counteracts the negative forces in our lives with God's positive force of His life-giving Word. It enables us to live in the positive power of God's truth, in His Word. It gives a sense of well-being never experienced before. It gives a sense that you are 'in' the world but not 'of' it. Unfortunately, the 'world' has much influence on our lives today, if we let it. "You do not belong to the world," Jesus said, "because My choice withdrew you from the world". *(John 15:19)*

The world will keep battering you no matter what. The evil one will always try and seek entry. The thief who comes to steal and plunder, won't easily give up on you. Learn to run to the Good Shepherd earlier for protection. Don't battle on, on your own. There's no need. "The world hates Me," Jesus tells us, "because I give evidence that its ways are evil." *(John 7:7)*

As His Word begins to take root in you, you will spot evil more quickly than ever before, you will not let it have power over you or steal your peace. "You will become wise as a serpent, and simple as a dove." *(Matthew 10:16)* Always remember Jesus has won the victory over the devil, over sin, over death. "Jesus has taken away all the power of the devil, by His death on the Cross." *(Hebrews 2:14)*

"The devil is a liar," *(John8:4)* "a thief," *(John10:9)* and "a murderer," *(John8:44)* Jesus tells us. He tries to deceive people, trapping them in negative thinking about themselves, so that this becomes the power in their lives rather than the power of God's Word. Jesus is Lord. He alone is Saviour.

He alone is the Healer who does not change, and who wants you alive! "Christ is the same, yesterday, today and forever." *(Hebrews 13:8)* He is alive today, hence we can ask Him to heal any time in our life where we have been hurt.

Focus on Him and His power to save. "Be fore-armed with the armour of God."
(Ephesians 6:14-17)
St. Paul encourages us to put this armour on every day for protection against the enemy and to be ready for the battle.

God's Word tells us the truth. It tells us who we really are in His sight. That should be all that matters to us. God longs to be of greatest importance in our lives. His Word will then mean everything to us. It is always alive and active, and when we apply it to our lives for healing, it will lead to undreamed of changes. It's fantastic! It costs nothing except your co-operation, for God's grace within you, is a free gift from Him.

If you live subject to the negative word, life can be very dull and unhappy. If you learn to live in the positive word, life can really be for living, and you yourself will be much happier. If you are already happy, you will experience even a deeper happiness. Negatives cause nothing but trouble though God can use them for greater growth for us. However, we must deal with them.

May I suggest you make a list of the negatives in your life. I mean the ones that

affect you badly. You must work at them by
applying God's positive Word of Scripture
to each one of them. It's well worth doing
this. It will pay dividends. God's Word is
always alive and active. It brings new life. If
you believe God's positive word and allow it
to counteract the negative word spoken
against you, you'll see great results. Hug
God's Word to your heart. The change you
will begin to see in yourself, is not an external
change. It will work from within outwards,
like a living fountain inside you, whose waters
never run dry. "The water I will give," said
Jesus, "will turn into a spring inside him,
welling up to eternal life" *(John 4:14)*

Living in the Word, will put you on another
plane of living, positively the best! You
must 'let' the Word change you from
within. No one can do this for you but
yourself. 'You' must believe in the power of
the Word. Then, any change in you, could
be a permanent change. People will see
the change in you and this will be a witness
to God's power at work in you. Never
under estimate the power of God's living
Word.

St. Paul tells us:
"The Word of God is something alive and

active: it cuts like any double edged sword
but more finely: it can slip through the
place where the soul is divided from the
spirit, or joints from the marrow; it can
judge the secret emotions and thoughts.
No created thing can hide from Him,
everything is uncovered and open to the
eyes of the One to whom we must give
account of ourselves." *(Hebrews 4:12-13)*
The possibility of improving our lives by
taking a 'fresh' look at them is indeed
exciting. The ability to 'let go' is a great
grace. The desire to change and become
more 'free in spirit', is yet a greater grace.

We all have people who could 'improve' us.
Some people want to change everyone else
except themselves. They think all must bow
to them! The truth is that most of us need
some inner healing at some time. However,
we like to think it's others who need it, not
us. Thank God there are no perfect
people. If there are, you're in trouble!

There's nothing worse than people thinking
they know you (when they don't), and they
know 'exactly' what you need (when they
can't cope with life too well themselves);
and they know how things should be done
for you, (when you have far more

experience of life and wit than they seem to
have ever had). Keep well out of these
people's way if you can, or else do as Jesus
said about the Pharisees, listen to them but
take no notice of them! God has a great
sense of humour and life can be very
amusing sometimes with Him. He seems to
have it all 'topsy turvy'. He chooses the
most unlikely people to do His work – even
important work – for Him. He chooses the
weak to confound the strong.

Listen to what Scripture says about this:
"It was to shame the wise that God chose
what is foolish by human reckoning, and to
shame what is strong that He chose what is
weak by human reckoning; those whom the
world thinks common and contemptible are
the ones God has chosen, those who are
nothing at all, to show up those who are
everything." *(1 Corinthians: 27-29)*

He will always give you comfort if someone
pulls you down. "If others bow you down,
He will raise you up." *(Psalm 145:14)*
Likewise, He will always give you the people
you need at the right time. He knows best!
He will use you elsewhere if someone is
trying to stop the good work you are trying to
do for Him in a particular place. He will not
be deterred or bound by anyone.

You must expect difficulties if you stand for goodness and truth. The apostles were constantly being attacked and even beaten up and imprisoned. Did you know that all, except Saint John the Evangelist, the beloved, were martyred for their Master Shepherd? They were all given a chance to show the depth of their love for Him. So, by walking with the Good Shepherd, of course you will have some hurdles. Perfectly normal! "Those who stand for Christ are bound to be attacked." *(2 Timothy 3:12)*

God's Mission Field is enormous. He can use you anywhere, at any time, just as you are. All He wants is a heart in love with His. Fortunately, He can use us in our brokenness too and often even because of it and in the most unexpected places, using us just as we are. I'm sure He would like our wholeness too! He sees to the heart of each soul every time. He is not a respecter of persons and has no favourites. "What I have come to realise is that God does not have favourites, but that anybody of any nationality who fears God and does what is right, is acceptable to Him." *(Acts 10:35)*

God is amazing how He sees everything. Nothing escapes Him! Do you ever have a little secret laugh with Him? I do!! Don't let anyone 'control' you - only the Lord Jesus. Some people seem to have a controlling spirit, and want to 'change' you, thinking they know what's best for you. If this happens in a marriage, it could be disastrous.

Go to the headquarters yourself first and deal with the top directly! That's what I do! Let Jesus the Lord, the Good Shepherd teach you. He'd like that! Let Him deal with you, teach you, change you, lead you to 'fresh' green pastures.

Let He Himself give you repose, in order to make life better for yourself and others. If you are a family person, please do your best in this area of change! We need 'healed' family people. The ripples will reach eternity! Ask Him to show you what needs changing in you. Ask Him to help you to change what 'you' have to change. "Abide in Me," He says, "Let My word make its home in you." *(John 15:7)*

Of course, He will co-operate with your plan to let His word dwell in you. He wants you to be your best self, that's why He came, remember? He gave His life, that you might live! No half measures. I think He likes you

to tell Him how you would like to change.
When I talk of your becoming your true self
don't misunderstand me. I'm not talking
here about an 'ego' trip, or selfishness or
self-centredness, or women's lib, or any
other lib, or disobedience, or anything like
that. I'm simply talking from the heart,
about the truth that seems to have been
denied so many people during their lives.

This is my experience from praying with
people, who are fortunately seeking a better
way of life. They've lived with such lies
about themselves and some tell me they
hate being trapped by negative words.
They want to 'break out' of this terrible
bondage put upon them in childhood or at
school or work and they don't seem able.

Of course with God's help and inner
healing they can. This is the best news.
Their spirit may be broken but they can
revive! I've seen it so often. "Though I go
through the bitter valley , You make it a
place of springs." *(Psalm 84:6)*
The Good News of the Gospel offers new
life. Jesus is the Healer, the only Healer,
and it is through His Death we are healed.
"Through His wounds we are healed."
(Isaiah 53:5)

We need to get life in perspective, God's perspective on you. I'm talking about you seeing yourself as you are and not as someone else sees you or wants to see you. "Will the real me please stand up?" is the title of an inspiring book by John Powell, S.J. So change and healing are about you, the 'real' you. The 'you' you long to be. The 'you' that has not yet been allowed to come to birth. The 'you' that has been stifled. The 'REAL' you!

Jesus can, if you let Him, walk you back in memory to heal your hurts. He has left you an inheritance that is yours. No one has a right to steal your inheritance from you, for through your Baptism, you become God's child. You are an heir to God's Kingdom. So believe in yourself. If you make Jesus Lord of your life, you can become more and more yourself and more and more healed and happy.

"Grow strong in the Lord, so that Christ may live in your hearts through faith, and then, planted in love and built on love, you will, with all the saints, have strength to grasp the length and breadth, the height and depth, until knowing the love of Christ, which is beyond all knowledge, you are

filled with the utter fullness of God.
Glory to Him, whose power working in us,
can do infinitely more than we can ask or
imagine. Glory be to Him from generation
to generation in the Church and in Christ
Jesus, for ever and ever Amen".
(Ephesians 3:14-21)

This passage sums up inner healing very
beautifully and its effect on your life.
Build your house on Rock, the Rock of
God's Word. He will anoint you with His
balm, just let Him! Give Him permission to
make you whole. He's always wanting to
free you!

There are definite reasons why we may
need Inner Healing. It could even be as a
result of 'slight' hurts or minor regrets, like
the 'If only's'. If there are 'unresolved'
hurts lurking around, particularly in the
subconscious, deeply buried, and you are
not one hundred per cent at peace with
yourself, that's a good enough reason. You
may not even be aware that you could have
a much happier life, with greater
appreciation of everything, greater
simplicity, until you see others who have
been freed. They seem to be so liberated in
the best sense of the word.

Hurts if not dealt with, can affect us adversely. "Refuse to brood over yesterday's and today's wounds", dear Brother Roger of Taizé used to say. You could waste your life away you know, and remain half alive, and some people unfortunately do. They live in the past most of the time. They never wake up to the present. Some remain stuck at a hurt or hurts that happened when they were children, and they find it impossible to break free of these hurts. The hurts in fact haunt them all their lives. The Good News for them is that they can part with these 'ghosts' and move on with the help of inner healing.

One woman I prayed with, told me she carried a hurt for sixty years and now she has been able, with the help of inner healing, to let it go. She came to a day for healing I was leading. I didn't actually pray over her. In fact, I didn't even have the opportunity to speak to her during the day. I merely prayed for healing over the whole group. During the prayer session, she had a spectacular spiritual healing and she received the great grace to forgive someone after sixty years. She is a new woman today as a result. Her letter to me is a treasure witnessing to the power of God's Word. What a witness! I have met her since, stayed in her lovely home and together we have given glory to God for this beautiful healing. Wonderful!

Have you heard the story of the Artist who wanted to paint the face of Christ, so he searched long and hard to find a beautiful face on a young man? He set to, found such a man and painted a wonderful picture.

Some years later, the Artist wanted, this time, to paint the sorrowing Christ. He sought high and low for a face of a man scarred with pain and sorrow in the gutter and deprived area of the city. He found such a man and painted a wonderful picture.

Later when he compared the two portraits he realised he had met and painted the very same man twice over! How circumstances had changed his appearance! What life can do to us if we let it!

Each drug addict, alcoholic, prostitute, murderer, thief, suicide bomber, has a story, of where it all went wrong for them. It is definitely known to the Good Shepherd! In fact we all have a story. Often our

weakness or even our sin, is partly the
result of the things that have hurt us and
made us vulnerable and broken of spirit.
We may not of course be aware of this!
Only God sees the whole picture, and the
mystery of what went wrong and why, and
why individuals behave in a particular way,
even to punishing their children because of
their own hurts. Others even punish
themselves by wayward behaviour because
they do not feel good enough to behave
normally. They sadly don't seem to think
they deserve any better. They might punish
innocent people too, like we've seen
recently with the growing evil of suicide
bombers at home and abroad. It is, as if
they have a grudge against the world, and
they feel they have to punish themselves
and others, because of 'unworthy' feelings,
even feelings of self-hate. Pray for them.

Not to love yourself is one of the greatest
diseases in today's world! These poor
people must hate themselves a lot, that's
why it all goes wrong for them, though
they're brain washed into thinking they are
doing a good job and they will become
heroes! Such need they have for the Good
Shepherd's wisdom, to know good from
evil, to hear the Gospel and to understand

the second commandment which says ' love
your neighbour as you love yourself'.

Even if you think you have had a good life
(like I did) there is always much more with
God and always better and richer pastures.
The 'secret' is within each of us and sadly
some people never find it. They look for
the answer elsewhere. In the book 'The Art
of Understanding Yourself'', Cecil Osborne
writes: "If there are inner conflicts and
tensions, anxiety and guilt, at some point in
his or her life, the individual will tend to
manifest this spiritual disease, by some
physical symptoms".

I believe much stress, depression, bitterness,
suffering, trauma, and illness, could be
lessened or avoided, if people only knew
where their present troubles were rooted,
and if they worked with the root cause for
healing. It is important to find the root
cause of the problem. Finding the root may
be a great surprise, as you may not connect
the problem with this particular root.

Sometimes when we're praying for healing
the Holy Spirit shows us the root very
quickly, and the healing that ensues is
instant and tremendous. Often a pattern

of behaviour sets up as a result of the first hurt (root), and we pray together to break this pattern in Jesus' name, thus liberating the person from it. Sometimes it takes a little co-operation on the part of the person healed, to work with their healing specifically for a little while, in case the evil one snatch away the truth.

The past experiences of hurts have quite a profound effect and stronghold on people's lives. To be 'open' to learning how to use the past constructively is indeed a great blessing, for with God nothing is wasted, not even our sin! We can vouch for this, by taking a look at the apostles and saints, and even some living 'saints' that we ourselves know today. To be able to readjust attitudes is a starting point to Inner Healing. God's grace enables! It is we who block it. We need to understand life's mystery more. Understanding leads to compassion, compassion leads to forgiveness, forgiveness leads to inner healing, inner healing leads to wholeness.

"Close to Me, their lives would lose their tension. It would be 'life together' with Me; I carrying the heavy end of things. Our hearts must merge. Isn't this the aim of My

Christians? You aren't bold enough. Some
are indifferent: Ponder on your poverty and
My richness. Tell Me about it. Ask the
Holy Spirit to brood over you as He
brooded over the waters before the end of
Creation." *('He and I', Gabrielle Bossis)*

Many a married couple (or person) tell me,
they would have loved to have known about
inner healing earlier in their lives seeing the
benefit it is to them now. They say how
different their lives might have been and
some of the hurts that have damaged their
relationship within their marriage, might
have been dealt with differently or even
averted. Some marriages might not even
have broken up either. However, let what
has happened be.

The most difficult thing in life is probably
relationships. Why we love this one and
can't stand that one, is a bit of a mystery,
isn't it? I suppose people enter into the
closest relationship of marriage with such
good will and excitement; they may have
been very young; or not known each other
very well or even not known each other at
all; believing their love would change
everything that is not perfect. If difficulties
arise, they hope their love will win through.

Sometimes people are totally incompatible but unfortunately they didn't see this before they ventured into marriage. Love does change everything, but 'we' can't change people. We can only change ourselves. It is a hard lesson to learn for all of us. When we change, everything changes, that is the miracle. A woman with great healing ministry in the USA was praying for her husband to change for eighteen years, but when she stopped praying for him to change and began to pray and change herself, she saw amazing changes in him!!

Didn't that wonderful dream come true
Maybe that was not meant for you
Lovely it seemed at its first bright glow
Didn't it last? Maybe let it go!
Learn to accept the things you can't change
For the pattern of life is not yours to arrange
And one day you'll laugh at those tears shed by you
All over a dream
That could never come true.
Anonymous

© Photograph Judy Fox

Where there's a Shadow there's a Light!

The Good Shepherd never stops re-inviting us to a better life. If there is hope of reconciliation, of starting again, do start, provided there is love, but if not, if love has grown cold, leave all in the hands of the Good Shepherd who understands.

He alone can bring good out of evil, and isn't it true that sometimes the saddest thing that has ever happened to us, might even become the best thing in the end. We think it is the end when in fact it is only the beginning.
Amazing how life goes. We have lovely plans sometimes that all go wrong! Mistakes happen! I was leading a seminar once in Bedford and this lovely 'old' couple came to it and they had just come back together after twenty years apart. Who knows?

No matter what has happened, we must try to move on. One loving old couple told me it was arguing that kept them together for fifty years! He said "If she says that's black, I'll say it's white!" Try to make the best of what is now. Be strong. We all know it's waste of time living with regrets. No use getting stuck, dwelling on the 'If only's'. That's a killer!

Thank God for now and for leading you to where you are today. He can turn bad to good for those who love Him. "We know that by turning everything to their good God co-operates with all those who love Him." *(Romans 8:28))* And again we read these comforting words: "Nothing can come between us and the love of Christ, even if we are troubled or worried, lacking food or clothes, or even attacked." *(Romans 8:35)*

Never waste time in regrets, what is, is now. We can't turn the clock back. With this type of healing, the ball is in your court. It is there for the taking. It's up to you now! You can't blame anyone else, if God has allowed what has happened so far in your life. He is giving you another chance now. 'He can turn thy winters to summers, though thou have no spring'. *(John Donne)*

Change can only come from within a person, no one else can change you. I know myself from changing my attitudes, how I've changed. So I saw myself, people, life, God, differently. Because my perception of myself changed, I found I began to live more fully, especially in areas of my life that were stifled or dormant. I began to like myself better. I liked other people better too!

Some people may see that we need to change, in a way we ourselves simply can't see. Other people again may see hurts dominating our lives They may see our potential stifled by our wrong attitudes to things, or to ourselves. They even may have been partly responsible for stifling us. Of course, if people really loved us enough, they would be positive in their attitudes to us and would wish us well and not be jealous. They would love to see us coming alive. No one ever wants to admit being jealous! They would always want to draw out our best, and be even delighted when we blossom.

Always put the best into life and you will get back the best! Put into life what you want to get out of it, treat others as you would like them to treat you. "So always treat others as you would like them to treat you." *(Matthew 7:12)* It always works! Spread love as best you can. Make this a priority.

"Transfiguration is not something we can achieve, it is something which only He who is mighty can bring about in us". *(Gerald Vann, O.P.).* Transfiguration happens to us! It is pure grace. Positive attitudes are vital for transfiguration. The danger with "negative" attitudes and "negative" words is that they stick like 'barnacles' and become so much part of us, that we almost believe they are true and that this is the 'real' us. In fact that's far from the truth, and deep down in our hearts we ourselves know this.

Unfortunately, we tend to let the negative word about ourselves dominate us too easily. If we hear negatives often enough, especially as a child, e.g. you're stupid, useless, can't do it, never will make it, not wanted, not as good as your brother or sister and so on, we'll absorb them and lose any bit of confidence we might have had. We know we're not the sum of these negatives and wish to be known as ourselves, but it doesn't seem to happen that way. It's as if we're put in a box labelled "STUPID" or "USELESS" and that's it forever. No use trying this one - Useless! The saying goes 'Give a dog a bad name and hang him'.

I find people long to be known for who they really are, and long to 'be themselves', they yearn to be released from these 'negative' traps but don't seem to be able to release themselves. They want to breathe but can't! I have Good News for them. What they really need is some inner healing. The Holy Spirit could and wants to do this for them. God wants us all to become ourselves, to become 'real'. "Of course I want to cure you! Be cured!" Jesus said to the leper. *(Matthew 8:3)*

Some of the first examples of success stories in this area is to look at some of the people Jesus chose as Apostles or close friends. It speaks for itself what Inner Healing did for those who became Jesus' friends. His love and acceptance really does transform!

However, some people can't cope with you when you receive healing and become 'real'. When the Holy Spirit came upon the Apostles at Pentecost and they were changed men, some people laughed at them suggesting; "They have been drinking too much new wine." *(Acts 2:13)* It makes people feel insecure! They cannot cope with your new found happiness, your enthusiasm for life, your ability to do things now. They would prefer you back in your box! Safer that way! More manageable!! They claim they want your happiness but when this inner healing happens to you and you become 'free' in your spirit, they are a bit lost! For one thing they can't control

you any more! They may even find it
difficult to relate to you after this. And this
is their loss!

To love someone is to let them go free.
"When Christ freed you, He meant you to
remain free." *(Galatians 5:1)* So be patient
and understanding with those on a different
wavelength to you just now. Let them be!
Mother Teresa used to say 'love till it hurts',
but I would say "You'll hurt, till you love."
God is love and that is all He has shown us.
So courage!

The only yardstick for change is Jesus. The
only way to change is to grow like Him. No
use having another human being as your
model. A waste of a life! Love must begin
within yourself first, then in your own
family, and then flow outwards to others.
So keep loving those who don't understand
you, especially at home! Keep praying that
eventually they will understand and benefit
from inner healing too!
Now all of us are conditioned in some way,
even without realising it. Many suffer as a
result of conditioning; and it is difficult to
break behaviour patterns especially if they
are linked to upbringing (except of course
by the power of The Holy Spirit). Guilt or

letting people down, would play a major
role here I believe. Indeed, we all agree
that a certain amount of conditioning is
necessary for training and good manners,
and for a good and caring life.

But with the London bombings recently,
we can see the evil effect of wrong
conditioning and brain washing. These
poor deluded suicide bombers not only took
their own lives (thinking they were doing a
service to Allah) but caused only evil,
destruction, loss of lives to many innocent
victims. What a work of satan! We know
that suffering is a part of life, but we also
know that the evil one causes much of it.

"The world hates Me", Jesus said,
"because I give evidence that its ways are
evil." (John 7:7)   No one escapes the
constant battle between good and evil. We
are in the world, but not of it. Jesus had
to remind His disciples. Same for us! The
struggle continues in all our lives till Christ
be formed in us, and till the end of time.

It is wonderful to read in the Old Testament
about Solomon, when God asked him what
he would like to have, and God was so
delighted with his request. Instead of asking

for long life for himself or riches or the lives of his enemies, Solomon asked God for a discerning judgement for himself and a heart to understand how to discern between good and evil. God gave him a heart wise and shrewd. *(cf. 1 Kings 3)*
This is exactly what suicide bombers need today, and all others who plot evil. People must not be intimidated by the work of the evil one.

Saint Francis de Sales says:

> "Do Not Fear what may
> happen tomorrow.
> The same loving Father
> who cares for you today
> will care for you tomorrow
> and everyday.
> Either He will shield you
> from suffering,
> or He will give you
> unfailing strength to bear it;
> Be at peace, then,
> and put aside all anxious
> thoughts and imaginings."

Our tragedy is not what we suffer – but what we don't learn from it when we do suffer. In retrospect, we see more clearly and see God's hand at work in it. Saint Francis de Sales

spoke of each person's tailor-made cross.
Doesn't God write straight with crooked
lines? Anything we suffer is of great
importance to our spiritual growth.

God is often blamed for the suffering in the
world but most of it, if we are honest, is
caused by human beings who abuse their
'free will'. The answer is not to take their
free will away from them but to pray and
hope that all human beings will have good
upbringing and be schooled in good rules of
behaviour and respect for other human
beings.

If our suffering is caused by rejection, we
can sometimes grow more through
rejection than through acceptance, because
acceptance could easily make us more
complacent, while rejection brings
awareness of the things in us that may need
change or correction. It also give us the
chance to identify with the Good Shepherd
and to suffer with Him, who experienced
such hostile rejection from His very own
people. A blessing to remember and for
which to thank Him! Bitter sweet! We
have to suffer with Him you know.
In a strange sort of way, the person who
does you the greatest favour in the long

run, is the one who disturbed your peace, rejected you, and brought out negative feelings. Though we don't like it, if we deal positively with these feelings, it could lead us to greater freedom! It's our own mistake if we let life make us bitter people:
"Be careful that no one is deprived of the grace of God, and let no root of bitterness begin to grow and make trouble; this can poison a whole Community." (Hebrews 12:15)

A person may likewise be rejecting in us some attribute they would long for in themselves, so they may see us as a threat to them. Unpleasant but true! They reject what they think we are, which may or may not be the truth! How do you feel when this happens to you? What do you do? How do you react?

And what of the latest trend - bullying? Has this ever affected you? I hear quite a lot about people being bullied especially at school and at work; some 'victims' come for prayer. People can even let themselves get ill over being bullied and have to stop work. Some even might have recourse to suicide. It's such an ugly thing, like sarcasm. Bullies are such cowards and such insecure people. They're so pathetic. Sadly it is becoming

the cancer of our society today, killing the
joy of life and friendship of work.

When our spirits are low or we feel unwell
or even a bit moody or depressed, (hardly
knowing why) remember we don't see
things correctly 'as they are' or in
perspective, we focus in on ourselves,
tending to see things in our 'blurred' light
rather than in Christ's undiminished light.
We revert to our earlier 'conditioning',
comfort ourselves with wrong attitudes for
security (false!), find it difficult to learn from
the situation and so we don't move on. A
growth opportunity missed!

To make a big decision about your life at
such a time can be disastrous. Try to be
better to yourself than that. Give yourself a
chance. Try Inner Healing first. When we
agree to deal with tensions and conflicts, to
let ourselves be changed, everything
changes and everything becomes more
positive and more beautiful. Seeing life out
of focus is far too common a happening.

And by the way, did you know that nothing can happen to you without the Good Shepherd knowing it, or even allowing it? He is in charge no matter what!

"By turning everything to their good, God co-operates with all those who love Him."
(Romans 8:28)

Remember Jesus suffered before you and for you. Get close to Him!

Psalm Twenty Three

CHAPTER FIVE

If I should walk
in the valley of darkness
no evil would I fear.

(Psalm 23:4)

A Clearer Perspective!

© Photograph Josephine Walsh

He'll set me free!

The Lord's My Shepherd, I'll not want,
He makes me down to lie
in pastures green. He leadeth me
the quiet waters by.

My soul He doth restore again,
and me to walk doth make
within the paths of righteousness
e'en for his own name's sake.

Yea, though I walk in death's dark vale,
Yet will I fear none ill.
For Thou art with me, and Thy rod
and staff me comfort still.

My table Thou hast furnishéd
in presence of My foes,
my head Thou dost with oil anoint
and My cup overflows.

Goodness and mercy all my life,
shall surely follow me.
And in God's house for evermore
my dwelling-place shall be.

(Paraphrase from Psalm 23)

PSALM TWENTY THREE

The Good Shepherd is calling us to a more intense belief in His daily Presence in our lives and in these words from Sacred Scripture.
"I am the same yesterday, today and forever." *(cf. Hebrews 13:8)*

I can hear Him say: 'Am I any different from yesterday? Do I love you for what you are worth or for your poverty? Can you not believe that I want your wholeness and fullness of life and that I alone can restore you? Learn from Me. Learn from life. Learn from nature. Look around you. See My creation. See Me at work in everything. Look to Me. Let nothing disturb you. I tell you, no rumours of evil, no evil from your

past, no hurtful or 'bad' memory, no menacing discord of our age, can ever drown out My voice. For as birds flying and eagles soaring, so will I, Your Good Shepherd, defend you and deliver you from all evil, within you and around you. I will preserve the music of your own being! Let the journey into Inner Healing fine tune you!'
"When all the strings of my life will be tuned, My Master, Your almighty Word will make the music of love resound." *(Tagore)*

We can learn so much by looking around us, by being aware, by seeing with a perceptive eye. I was once giving a day on Inner Healing and Healing of Memories in Manchester, the venue being a lovely junior school hall. Looking around, my eye was drawn to the fascinating display of children's work on the walls. Firstly, behind me, there were the Jacobean Memories, then to my right and in front, there were the Invaders and the Settlers. Perfect,166 I thought to myself, if this isn't linked to Inner Healing, I don't know what is! Couldn't be better! Such an aid to the day's theme.

The Jacobean memories, I suggested, represented our past; even our inherited difficulties, that plague some families, with tendencies passed down the family line from one generation to the next and needing "family tree" healing. Examples could be illnesses, physical or mental; depression, schizophrenia, suicide, fear, alcoholism, divorce, even a spirit of murder, hatred, unforgiveness, revenge, abortion, etc.

Curses too may have been passed down or may be put on families or an individual in a family. Where this has happened, we need to break the curse in the name of Jesus three times (always use His authority), thus setting the family free.

Some would have memories from childhood that affected them adversely. In fact, we all have some bad hurtful memories. No one escapes, even if you have had the best upbringing in the world. So you may need inner healing because of who you are (boy or girl) or where you come in the family, or what happened to you as a child. A parent could have been ill or the child separated from the mother or father. You could have had problems at birth or in the womb. Maybe your mother died at birth, or you were a twin and the other twin was stillborn and you were never told you were a twin and you find yourself always looking for something. Best tell a child the truth. Don't hide things because it causes too much trouble later on in life. That's my advice to you from my experience of praying with people over many years. "The truth will set you free." *(John 8:36)* Skeletons in the cupboard have a habit of falling out, or getting smelly if they don't !

Some memories will be so suppressed (so hurtful that you couldn't reach them) your psyche would not even want to own them. There is no need to dig them up. God knows all. He knows your deepest needs. Simply ask the Holy Spirit what is needed. He will help you. I can vouch for that. It is excellent to have Masses offered for Family Tree Healing. You could have been in an accident or been the victim of an unfortunate incident; better forgotten, you think. *(I think better out, not suppressed!)*

You may have been treated badly, you or a parent could have been the victim of violence, maybe through alcoholism. You may have been brought up with absence of a father, this may have caused insecurity. The problem may have been where you were brought up, with the family or apart.

'Break, break, break, on thy cold grey stones Oh sea, and I would that my tongue could utter the thoughts that arise in me'
(Alfred Lord Tennyson)

'Only love melts and heals'
(cf 1 John)

Winter…

Maybe you had too many critical (even rude and vulgar words) thrown at you and some have got 'stuck' so that you don't really know who you are.

Don't believe these negative words any more, let your mind become enlightened through the living power of God's Word for you. It's the only Word worth listening to. It's the Word that will give you life because it is the Truth; all these things and more, can affect us as human beings. We are amazingly sensitive. Not much escapes our unconscious memory. It's like a tape recorder. It misses nothing.

Hence the need for the positive upbuilding word to your child if you are a parent. Praise goes much further than criticism, especially with children, and has a much better effect. The only thing I remember from the lovely Bambi film, is Bambi saying: "If you can't say something nice, say nothing at all." It would be a different world for most people, if this happened, especially in their upbringing. I find many people are hurt because of upbringing.

Then I considered The 'Invaders'. These I thought could be all the bad things that happen to us, that bombard us and affect us.

Some invaders may have an appearance of
good, but in fact are not.
Among the invaders are the negative words,
ugly treatment, being overlooked, ignored,
teased, unloved, called names, pushed
down, pushed out of the way; out of sight
out of mind, forgotten, locked in a room,
put in a black hole, punished unjustly, too
strict an upbringing, told you'd never be any
good, you could never do anything right,
attacked by evil, used in satanic worship,
abused sexually, mocked, shouted at
frequently, sworn at, discriminated against,
treated without respect, without security,
childhood stolen, punished too harshly,
beaten, condemned unjustly, pulled from
pillar to post, maybe because of divorced
parents, compared with others, put in a
home, adopted or fostered (only of course if
it went wrong), not fed properly, sent to
bed hungry, deprived or cheated of an
inheritance, deprived of contact with
relatives, deprived of your faith inheritance.

There are so many 'invaders', some more
dangerous than others, some that hurt
more deeply than others, some
unfortunately that leave their mark for life,
some that leave you with many fears; even
inordinate fears.

A person might have one or none or a few
of these things happen to them, but in my
praying with people for inner healing, I
hear of so many invaders, that I decided to
list them here in case a bell rings for you. I
can see how these 'invaders' become
'settlers' and in fact they can and do cause a
lot of trouble and unnecessary misery in
people's lives and they can be dealt with so
easily with inner healing without all the
trauma of endless counselling and expense.
Life is too short to be stuck with these
negatives when we know Jesus wants us to
have a beautiful life. The Holy Spirit is so
gracious! There are so many success
stories, that I hope if you read this book, it
will help you and encourage you to go for
inner healing if needed. I will show you
here how you yourself can pray for your
own healing. God will help you. He is
always waiting to restore our brokenness.

Some people tell me of 'invaders' that have
had disastrous effect on their lives, how
they feel 'dead' inside and disturbed and feel
so broken especially from the past, that
they wished certain things had not
happened to them because they can't get
going. They long for a life, for peace of
mind. This is exactly what the Good

Shepherd does for them through inner healing. It's so beautiful. He picks them up, carries them like His lambs close to his breast, and restores them to peace. They begin to hear the music of their own being at last. The years the locusts have stolen can be restored in Him.

This is the Good News, that the light of the Holy Spirit, and prayer for inner healing, can change the 'recall' of bad memories, so that they do not hurt so much any more. When healed fully they do not hurt at all! What's happened can't change but the effect of what's happened and the pain of it all, can be different. Jesus can anaesthetise the pain and deep wound, and He can go back to your past and heal the places where the hurt has been.

Healing is possible. We can have a new start. "I will place a new spirit within you and I will give you a new heart." *(Ezekiel 36:26)* Patterns of behaviour can be broken, especially those emerging as a result of the 'invaders'. The root of the problem is often revealed by the Holy Spirit and dealt with miraculously by Him. When His healing balm is applied all becomes fresh. "Fresh and green are the pastures where He gives me repose, near restful waters He leads me, to revive my drooping spirit." *(Psalm 23)* I've witnessed grace so often.

There is no reason why 'invaders' should become 'settlers', neither must we let them. "If I should walk in the valley of darkness, no evil would I fear. You are there with your crook and your staff, with these you give comfort." *(Psalm 23:4)* Learn to keep your eyes on the Good Shepherd.

A plea to parents to keep an open mind on Inner Healing. Everyone knows how hard it is to bring children up well today. Though many parents do their best for their children, we all make mistakes and it is amazing how even the smallest incident can have such dire consequences for a child, because unfortunately hurts stick. Human beings are so vulnerable.

Parents do not realise how they hurt their children sometimes. Often they've been hurt by their own up bringing, and so unfortunately continue the same pattern with their own children.

Because a child has an innate love for a parent, they tend to cover up for the parent, make excuses for them, never want to hurt them, or blame them. There is a sacredness about this relationship, and that's why it is very sad when anything goes wrong. Part of the problem is the child's inability to extricate themselves from this tie in order to get healing. Sometimes they think they might be letting their parents down if they say anything negative about them.

It's not a question of allocating blame, the important thing is to help the person you are praying with to get healing. If you are praying for someone, you don't want to come between the love of a child and a parent: on the contrary, one would normally pray for the strengthening of this bond between them.

The secret of inner healing is to allow God's Love to restore and bring healing. Forgiveness is always the key.

My friend, C…, explained beautifully: "You know how my husband had been unfaithful to me, but the moment I forgave him from my heart I found peace. No matter what he will do now, after my forgiving him, it won't hurt me. You see, Josephine, you have to cross the Rubicon. Once you have crossed

over the bridge leading from unforgiveness
to forgiveness, you then have to destroy it
there behind you and leave it in pieces. If
you want to forgive there's no going back.
So I forgave. And now I have new life. It's
all grace, Josephine. Jesus is wonderful!"

If you can't forgive, it is important that you
give Jesus permission to forgive for you.
Only grace can do this. It is always God
Himself who heals a person, never a human
being! Human beings can be but channels
of God's healing power. The Good
Shepherd never deserts His sheep. You
can always rely on Him even if he appears
to be asleep (as in the boat when the
apostles seemed to be drowning). *(cf.
Matthew 8:25)* Give Him a chance!

If you invite Jesus into the hurt memory and
past situation (or present one). Talk to
Jesus about it. Imagine it as vividly as you
can. Ask Him to help you to forgive and to
let go of the hurt, and place the hurt at the
foot of the cross (the victory ground) by
giving it to Jesus. His grace of forgiveness
is always there for the taking. Don't be
blinded by hurt emotions. Forgiveness is of
the will irrespective of the temperature of
the emotions. Then in Jesus' name, you

'The rich meadow grass seemed that morning of a freshness and a green unsurpassible!'
*('Wind in the Willows':
Kenneth Grahame)*

A shoot springs from the stock of Jesse!
(Isaiah 11:1)

Spring ...

must cut the links not of God in any relevant relationship. Ask Jesus to restore the brokenness to wholeness and pray for the in-filling of the Holy Spirit. It's amazing what the Holy Spirit does in this type of prayer. If praying with a parent, I ask them to give a mother's or a father's blessing to the child concerned, then seal all in the precious blood of Jesus.

I saw the 'Settlers' as the unhealthy attitudes, unhelpful, negative words spoken against us, that become like barnacles that stick hard, and are very hard to shift. They become embedded in our unconscious. We may not even know about them (but God does and so does your psyche). They do not want to move! Some have been there for so long they need the equivalent of a pick axe to move them. They may have disastrous effects on people's personalities, making them feel depressed, unclean, rejected, a nuisance, unloved, insecure. Hence as a result of the 'settlers', people could turn to drugs, drink, all sorts of permissive behaviour, vandalism, theft, violence etc., as false comfort.

We had a Nigerian priest staying with us at our Convent in Olney. One day he had offered to help us by doing the washing up and he was furiously scrubbing the pots and pans. When we told him to leave them and not be too fussy, he replied, "This bit does not belong to the pot!" and he kept on scrubbing – *(the barnacles!)*.

We become what we're not, because of things that happen to us which mar our beauty and do not really belong to us. These things must be dealt with. Our inheritance is, I repeat, that we are heirs of God, that we are His children and our true inheritance is love, peace, goodness and right living. God's love is the enabler. Have you thanked Him?

Always remember that the Good Shepherd loves us unconditionally. He wants us to know more and more that we are His, and that He has plans for us. That we are his favourites. "I have plans for you, plans for your welfare not your woe." *(Jeremiah 29:11)* We're very slow learners, slow to know his love and even slower to believe in it. We need to learn to receive His love. It's pure gift. Always available! He has made us part of a great inheritance, and all we can do is to bow down in adoration before Him, and thank Him for all His great love and

care for us. There's no one like Him.
These are the sort of settlers you must
encourage to stay. They are by far the
best!

This leads me to the last part of this chapter
which I hope will help you. You can add to
it by yourself as the Lord gives you the
Scriptures appropriate to you. Work with
your own inner healing as the Scriptures
light up for you.

Get good at applying God's Word, the
positive Word of power to your situations.
I'm sure there must be a positive Word of
God for every negative word we experience
in life, just as I believe there must be a cure
for all illnesses in nature. God would never
have made an incomplete world.

First of all you must deal with the negative
words. These have caused you pain, and
been destructive to you. Some commonly
used negative words and phrases are listed
on page 190 -199, and on the opposite
pages are the positive Words of Scripture.
Take the negative word, rebuke it in Jesus'
name, revoke it, renounce it in His Name.
Read the opposite positive Word of
Scripture to yourself several times (if

necessary) till it sinks in, till you start believing it, the truth of who you are before God. No harm to quote these words to satan, 'the accuser', since you can see how Jesus himself dealt with him, and he does try to trap us in negatives. When he had the cheek to tempt Him in the desert, Jesus' armour was the Word of God which He quoted to the evil one. "Begone satan!" Jesus said, "you will not tempt the Lord your God, and Him only will you serve."

You know God's Word from Scripture:

> *"Unload all your worries onto Him since He is looking after you. Be calm and vigilant, because your enemy the devil is prowling around like a roaring lion looking for someone to eat. Stand up to him, strong in the faith, and in the knowledge that your brothers all over the world, are suffering the same things. You will have to suffer only for a little while: the God of all graces, who called you to eternal glory in Christ, will see that all is well again. He will confirm, strengthen, and support you. His power lasts forever and ever. Amen"*
> *(1 Peter 5:7-11)*

So let the Word of God dwell in your heart like a mantra. It is powerful. Any time you feel tempted to feel a negative thought especially against yourself, keep repeating the Word of Scripture, the 'power' Word.

Try it! The power of Scripture is superb. Let God's Word do the job for you. It tells us in Scripture that His Word never goes back to Him empty. Eventually then it will become so much part of you that almost automatically this will happen for you.

> *"In receiving the word from us, you received not a human word but the Word of God which is now at work in you."*
> *(1 Thessalonians 2:13)*

"Yes, as the rain and the snow come down from the heavens, and do not return without watering the earth, making it yield and giving growth to provide seed for the sower and bread for the eating, so the Word that goes from my mouth does not return to me empty, without carrying out My will and succeeding in what it was sent to do." *(Isaiah 55:11)*

God's Word has to be life giving because it is a Living Word. Let the **positive** Words of Scripture sink into your being. Let it counteract every negative word, and try not to use negative words in conversation yourself. We all do but we need to stop. I do too! Negative words can be very destructive.

"The Spirit you received is not a spirit of slaves bringing fear into your lives again; it is the spirit of sons and daughters, and it makes us cry out, Abba, Father!"
(Romans 8:16)

Build a better world of positive words. Help yourself to become healed by obeying God's Word. Listen to it and keep it in your heart as Mary did. "His Mother kept all these words and pondered them in her heart." *(Luke 2: 52)* She was so beautiful. She could say: "All generations will call me blessed, for He who is mighty has done great things for me". *(Luke 1:48)*
You will soon be saying: 'He who is mighty has done great things for me!' Can't wait!

Don't believe untruths about yourself any more. Come before Him humbly and magnify His name, for He has done wonders for you. Bless Him all the time.

'Never had they noticed the roses so vivid; the willow herb so riotous; the meadowsweet so odorous'
('Wind in the Willows': Kenneth Grahame)

'Of His fullness we have all received' (Prologue of St. John 1:16)

Summer...

With His strength in you, instead of saying
"I can't" you'll say "I can"; instead of
saying "I'm no good, I can't do it; you'll say
"I am good because God made me. I can
do all things in Him." So you could be
amazed at what you can do; instead of
saying "I'm unwanted, you can say: "My
Beloved is mine and I am His."
(The Song of Songs 2:16)

He says to us: "Place you heart in Mine in
joy as in distress. If I fill your cup to
overflowing, I am your peace. If I put you
to the test, I am your companion." How
He longs for us to be close to Him in all
things, and at all times!

Again, for example, when you feel ugly,
you can tell yourself: "For had You hated
anything, You would not have formed it."
(Wisdom 11:25). When you feel unable to
speak out, you know He will give you the
words to say, so take courage. Live!
Change! Go for the New Life! The World
is yours! Spread the Good News of Jesus.
Never stop proclaiming Him. Live for Him
and you'll live! Give up all this moaning
and self pity, and offer Him every little pain
even the secret ones!
Get conditioned by God's Word, not by
any one else's. Remember Jesus is Truth.

Only His truth can set you free. "If He sets you free, you are free indeed." (*Galatians 5:1*) Believe it!

"My chosen one in whom my soul delights." (*Isaiah 41:2*) How does this word make you feel? Can you believe it? That's you! "No need to recall the past." (*Isaiah 43:18*) Can you let your guilt go forever? Will you believe this word? Stop blaming yourself.

> "*You are all so ignorant of the power of your God. Are you afraid to know Him, you who seek Him so little? And yet the joy of your soul lies in constant communion with your Creator and Saviour, in the Christ-consciousness.*
> *Abandon yourself to God no matter what He does. Let His breath blow you along, fanned by your fervour. Come to Him eagerly My child, since He has the answers to all your needs: of tenderness, rest, intelligence. Your thoughts are short, but at least prolong your desires, so that you can reach a higher plane; the new heights where the spirit is waiting for you, to help you to climb higher.*" ('He and I', Gabrielle Bossis, pp.221-2)

It is a shame more people are not introduced to Inner Healing. It is like the narrow gate Jesus talks about, and few find it. But better find it a bit late than never! I hope you won't miss it; and having found it, I hope you will open this door to many others too. It is part of God's feast of Joy!

Good News is always for sharing. That's why I long to see people healed in this way. I long for the day when every parish will have a small team of people who will regularly minister Inner Healing to the community. There is no need to become so weary on the way that we cannot cope with life. We belong together and a problem shared is a problem halved. My prayer is for more and more growth in this ministry of Inner Healing, until we become more like Christ, transformed by His healing love to become our 'real' selves.

Of His Fullness ...!

Drench my spirit, Lord!

'Cascading Waterfall'

Love transforming, love restoring,
like a torrent cascading down.
Mountain peaks and rock-face layering,
drenched with healing, cleansing spray.
Cup of suffering, overflowing,
darkness lightened in His Will.
Faces drenched in radiant glory,
As His Healing now begins.

To help you get started in applying God's Word to yourself.

Now I'd like to help you with some Scripture passages to enable you to start on your own journey to Inner Healing. The route is via the Word of God only. You can start straightaway to counteract your own Negative words spoken by you or against you with God's Positive Words spoken to you in Scripture. I have helped you get started with some examples. Repeat the positive Scripture Words often to yourself, until you become convinced, re-conditioned by them. You must actually believe them in your regard. God's Word will become a mighty power within you.

You can continue to make up your own list by searching the Scriptures by yourself, or search with a friend. Time well spent! In the past you've been conditioned by negative words. Now you must come against negative words so as to be re-conditioned with positive words: "The truth will set you free"! *(John 8:32)*

If you persevere, it could be for you a life-changing experience forever. Then you have won!

You're good for nothing   ... ...

You're stupid ... ...

You should have been a boy!   ... ...

Self Condemnation   ... ...

I can't! Feel so inadequate ... ...

I feel inferior, fear of failure   ... ...

"We are God's Work of Art, created in Christ Jesus to live the good life He meant us to live." *(Ephesians 2:9)*

"I will instruct you and teach you the way you should go I will watch over you and be your adviser." *(Psalm 32:8)*
"You have made man little less than a god, with glory and honour you crowned him." *(Psalm 8:5)*
"I'm God's Child." *(1 John 3:1)*

"He made them male and female in His image." *(Genesis 1:27)*
"It was You who created me in my mother's womb." *(Psalm 139:13)*

"No condemnation in Christ Jesus." *(Romans 8:1)*

"I can do all things in Him who strengthens me." *(Philippians 4:13)*
"God chose the foolish to confound the strong." *(1 Corinthians 1:27)*

"My grace is enough for you." *(2 Corinthians 12:9)*

| I can't forgive myself ... ... |

| I'll never be forgiven ... ... |

| I can't speak out ... ... |

| I'm afraid ... ... |

| I'm so bitter ... ... |

| I feel so unloved ... . |

| I never felt loved by anyone ... ... |

.. ...   "I will never remember their sins." *(Hebrews 10:17)*

.. ...   "Happy the man whose fault is forgiven, whose sin is blotted out." *(Psalm 37:4)* "Neither do I condemn thee. Go, sin no more." *(John 8:11)*

.. ...   "Do not be afraid to speak out. I am with you." (Jeremiah. 1:6-8)
          "Do not be afraid to speak out or allow yourself to be silenced" (Acts 18:9)

.. ...   "You need not fear the terror of the night" *(Psalm 91:5)*
          "God's gift was not a spirit of timidity, bringing fear into your life but of power." *(2 Timothy 1:7)*

.. ...   "Watch out for bitterness... that no bitterness take root among you." *(Hebrews 12:15)*

.. ...   "I love you with an everlasting love." *(Jeremiah 31:16)*

.. ...   "God loved the world He sent His only Son to save it." *(John 3:16)*

I feel so guilty … … … … … … … …

I'm anxious and worried… … … … …

I don't belong anywhere   … … … …

I am rejected   … … … … … … … …

I feel so lonely … …… … … … … …

"No need to recall the past" *(Isaiah 43:18)*
"I admit my guilt. I am sorry for having sinned" *(Psalm 38:18)*

"There is no need to be anxious if you need any thing pray for it" *(Philippians 4:6)*
"No need to worry, Jesus said." *(Luke 12:25)*

"You are mine" *(Isaiah 44:2)*
"I called you by name. *(Isaiah 42)*
"He knows about everyone everywhere" *(Hebrews 4:13)*
"Every hair on your head have been counted. There's no need to be afraid" *(Luke 12:8)*

You're in good company Jesus was so rejected. "You are Mine" *(Isaiah 42:1)*
"In your old age I shall still be the same, I will support you. I will support you and deliver you. I have done so already. *(Isaiah 46:4)*

"I am always with you." *(Matthew 28:20)*
"Those who believe are never alone in life or in death." *(Pope Benedict XVI)*
"God is ever ready to help in times of trouble" *(Psalm 46:1)* "He has rescued us out of the gloom." *(Psalm 147:3*

I'm so depressed ... ...

I don't want to live ... ...

Regrets. I wish I hadn't ... ...

I deserve to be punished ... ...

I can't let go ... ...

. ...   "He has taken us out of the power of darkness and created a place for us in the Kingdom of the Son that He loves and in Him we gain our freedom, the forgiveness of our sins." *(Colossians 1:13-14)*

. ...   "Shattering their chains!" *(Psalms 107:14)*
"Breaking bronze gates open!" *(Ibid: 16)*
"He snatched them from the Pit, He sent his Word and cured them." *(Ibid: 20)*
"I have faith even when I say I am completely crushed." *(Psalm 116:10)*

. ...   "He cleanses us and gives peace." *(Colossians 2:15)*

. ...   "God forgives all our offences." *(Psalm 103:3)*
"God never treats us as our sins deserve, He never punishes us." *(Psalm 103:10)*

. ...   "Forgetting the past and looking forward to what lies ahead." *(Philippians 3:13)*

197

I'm ashamed   ... ...

I wish I were dead   ... ...

You're told you are a mistake   ... ...

You were never wanted   ... ...

. ....
"I admit my guilt." *(Psalm 37:4)*
"Every face turned towards Him grows
brighter and is never ashamed." *(Psalm 34:5)*
"Yahweh, my encircling shield you help
me hold up my head." *(Psalm 3:3)*
"You will forget the shame of your youth."
(Isaiah 54:4)

. ...
"When I am weak then I am strong." *(2
Corinthians 12:10)*
"He has rescued me from all my troubles."
(Psalm 54:7)
"When I call when I am in trouble, you
come to my relief." *(Psalm 54:4)*

. ...
"I formed you in the womb." *(Isaiah 43:7)*
"You are mine." *(Isaiah 43:1)*

. ...
"I carved you on the palm of my hand."
(Isaiah 49:16)
"Before you were in the womb I called
you." *(Isaiah 44:2)*
"You hold nothing of what you have made
in abhorrence." *(Wisdom 11:24)*

I hope you will have found some of these
Scripture texts appropriate for yourself and
should one or more of the negatives ring a
bell for you, I pray you will have the grace
and courage to believe only God's positive
word for you instead of the negatives.
Work hard at this. It's better than any
insurance policy and it will certainly improve your general health!

I cannot recommend enough the use of God's
Word. Let it become an integral part of your
daily life. We must become re- conditioned
by the positive 'power' word of God. If you
make a habit of repeating these verses of
Scripture and I'm sure God will give you
others, you will not only become familiar with
them, but you will have a new life-giving
source of energy in your life.

"I opened my mouth; He gave me the scroll
to eat and said: 'Son of man, feed and be
satisfied by the scroll I am giving you.' I ate,
and it tasted sweet as honey." *(Ezekiel 3:1-3)*
The scroll represents the word of God. It
creates energy, like honey, but it is totally
free! You can devour it!

Jesus called His word the seed. Never
forget that the seed germinates in the dark,

steadily, slowly and quietly, and when nothing 'seems' to be happening, that's actually when it all is beginning.

When you feel quite helpless, and you want change instantly, just be a little bit patient and give the seed a chance! Something good is always worth waiting for. Your most difficult time, may even be your best time in the end.

The seed falls on different soils and produces at different rates. Sometimes people have one very bad year when everything seems to be wrong, and they find it hard to cope with life. There is a saying 'one sorrow never comes alone'.

The seed seems to be dead. Give it a chance. Nurture it. Nourish it. Be persevering with it. As you learn to wait upon Gods' seasons of your life, His plan will unfold and the reasons why may emerge too.

The most painful year, to your surprise, may become your most liberating year for you, like my 1981. This was the worst year of my entire life, when I lost both my parents together, within two months of each other, with fourteen years difference between them in age!

But God knew best, and He, in spite of all the prayer or maybe perhaps because of it, saw best to take them home together, their work for Him done. Of course we didn't want to let them go, but I couldn't imagine them living without each other. His will be done!

Allow yourself to dig deep, turn over, pause to reflect, fertilize the soil of your soul, with His ever present mercies. God does not need our activity, He needs our hearts. That is why sometimes He woos us into the wilderness to speak to our hearts *(cf. Hosea 1:16)* and in the wilderness nothing seems to be happening, like the seed in the ground, silent, dormant, but God could be working mightily in us. One day is like a thousand years to Him. "To You, a thousand years are a single day, a yesterday now over, an hour of the night." *(Psalm 90:4)* He is always waiting for us, we are always in a hurry. He enforces a stillness upon us, as we learn to wait upon His seasons of our life.

Just as an athlete trains by doing exercises, so too must we train ourselves spiritually.

"Physical exercises are useful enough, but the usefulness of spirituality is unlimited since it holds out the reward of life here and now, and of the future life as well. "Your mind must be renewed by a spiritual revolution, so that you can 'put on' the 'new' self that has been created in God's ways, in goodness and holiness of the truth."
(Ephesians 4:23-24).
"New wine must be put into fresh skins, and both are preserved," Jesus said. *(Matthew 9:17).*

Why not decide again today to live for Him. You could do nothing better.

> "Let my heart live for you.
> My Spirit will live for you alone.
> You will cure me and give me life.
> My suffering will turn to health."
> *(Isaiah 38:16)*

'Jesus said to the woman with the haemorrhage, "Courage my daughter, your faith has restored you to health." And from that moment, the woman was well again.'
(Matthew 9:22) Do you hear Him telling you to have courage also because you are not alone? His presence is with you. He alone will heal you. Trust Him.

If we are serious about our spiritual life,
inner healing is a must. Many of us could
take God's word to heart a bit more, and
try to let it speak to us more powerfully
each day. We could get into the habit of
counteracting negative words with God's
Words more quickly, and not let the negatives take root. You know the negatives are
not true about you most of the time anyway, so why bother believing them. If
there is any truth in any of the negatives do
something about it, if not, why waste time
on what might be destructive to you? Time
is precious remember. Life is short. Listen
to your Good Shepherd. All the answers
you need are there in Scripture. Our faith
in God's Word can restore us to health. We
get bogged down by this and that, by this
attitude and that, and waste a lot of 'living'
time.

The Good Shepherd is constantly calling us
to a fuller and better life, healed by His
Word. Best listen to Him! Be ready for
everything. Never blame God when things
go wrong. By now you should know
where evil and negatives come from, they
certainly do not come from our loving God
and Good Shepherd. Try to get things in
perspective, God's perspective.

'Season of mists
and mellow
fruitfulness!'
(John Keats)

'Still full of sap,
still green, still
bearing fruit in old
age'
(Psalm 91)

Autumn ...

**"There is a season for everything,
a time for every occupation
under Heaven."**
(Ecclesiastes 3:1)

"A time for giving birth,
a time for dying;
a time for planting,
a time for uprooting
what has been planted.

A time for killing,
a time for healing;
a time for knocking down,
a time for building.

A time for tears,
a time for laughter;
a time for mourning,
a time for dancing.

A time for throwing stones away,
a time for gathering them up;
a time for embracing,
a time to refrain from embracing.

A time for searching,
a time for losing;
a time for keeping,
a time for throwing away.

A time for tearing,
a time for sewing;
a time for keeping silent,
a time for speaking.

A time for loving,
a time for hating;
a time for war,
a time for peace.

What does a man gain for efforts
that he makes? I contemplate the
task that God gives mankind to
labour at. All that he does is apt
for its time; but though He has
permitted man to consider time in
its wholeness, man cannot com-
prehend the work of God from
the beginning to end."

(Ecclesiastes 3:2-11)

He uses all times and all seasons for His
purpose and for your good, for His glory.
So give: "Glory to Him, whose power
working in us can do infinitely more than
we can ask or imagine; glory to Him from
generation to generation in the Church, and
in Christ Jesus for ever and ever. Amen."
(Ephesians 3:20-21)

PSALM TWENTY THREE

All Times Are His Seasons

God made the sun and moon to distinguish
seasons,
and day and night,
and we cannot have the fruits of the earth
but in their seasons;
But God hath made no decree to distinguish
the seasons of His mercies.
In paradise the fruits are ever at their maturity.
God never says you should have come
yesterday;
He never says you must come again tomorrow,
But today He will hear you.
He brought light out of darkness,
not out of lesser light;
He can bring thy summer out of winter
though thou have no spring.
All occasions invite His mercies
And all times are His seasons.
(John Donne - 1572-1631)

And by the way,
never forget that the Good
Shepherd is Omniscient,
so He knows all about you
and still loves you!
He will never change
in His love for you.
You can utterly rely on His
Faithfulness.
All occasions invite His
mercies.
All times are His seasons!

Psalm Twenty Three

CHAPTER SIX

You have prepared a banquet
for me in the sight of my foes
My head you have anointed
with oil, my cup is
overflowing.

(Psalm 23:5)

INVITATION

... ...

to the
Lord's
Celebration
Banquet

*'My Invitation is for every
man, woman and child!'*

The King of love My Shepherd is,
whose goodness faileth never;
I nothing lack if I am His
and He is mine forever.

Where streams of living water flow
my ransomed soul He leadeth,
and where the verdant pastures grow
with food celestial feedeth.

Perverse and foolish oft I strayed
but yet in love He sought me,
and on His shoulder gently laid,
and home, rejoicing, brought me.

In death's dark vale I fear no ill
with Thee, dear Lord beside me;
Thy rod and staff my comfort still,
Thy cross before to guide me.

Thou spread'st a table in my sight,
Thy unction grace bestoweth:
and O what transport of delight
from Thy pure chalice floweth!

And so through all the length of days
Thy goodness faileth never;
Good Shepherd, may I sing Thy praise
within Thy house for ever.

(Henry Williams Baker (1821-77)

PSALM TWENTY THREE

I am drawn to St. John's Gospel, chapter 6, where Jesus calls Himself the 'Bread of Life'.

"I am the Bread of Life, He who comes to Me will never be hungry; He who believes in Me will never thirst." *(John 6:35)* What a promise from our Good Shepherd!

Jesus continues:

"I am the living bread that has come down from Heaven. Anyone who eats this bread will live forever, and the bread that I shall give is My flesh for the life of the world." *(John 6:51)*

The banquet Jesus is talking about in Psalm 23:5 is intimately linked with communion and with union with Him. The anointing signifies respect and a welcome to the banquet, "My head you have anointed with oil." *(Psalm 37:4)*

Jesus, remember, was at Bethany at the house of Simon the Leper, shortly before His Passion.   He was anointed by Mary with the most expensive ointment, which she poured on His head as He was at table. The disciples present were indignant and thought this ointment was a waste of money, but Jesus thought differently!

Jesus was so touched by what she had done for Him at this meal, that He said: "I tell you solemnly, wherever in all the world this Good News is proclaimed, what she has done will be told also in remembrance of her. What she has done for Me, is one of the good works indeed! When she poured this ointment on My body, she did it to prepare Me for burial." *(Matthew 26:6-13)*

It was a prophetic sign, though unknown to her or any of the disciples. Now all the scriptures are fulfilled in Jesus and these words from Psalm 23, "My head you have anointed with oil, My cup is overflowing", could well be foretelling the terrible events to come in Jesus' life, His Agony in the

Garden of Gethsemane, His Passion and
His Crucifixion. Might the 'overflowing
cup' mean the overwhelming suffering
Jesus would soon have to face? "If this cup
cannot pass by without My drinking it, then
your will be done" was Jesus' prayer in
Gethsemane, to His Father. *(Matthew 26:42)*

It is more generally thought that the
'Banquet' represents the mystery of the
Eucharist, the overflowing cup representing
God's abundant giving. It is the mystery of
faith, the banquet where one receives the
precious Body of Christ, the Banquet of the
Lamb, where one will never be hungry. For
having found Christ, one has found
everything. There is nothing more. He is
our food and drink for life.
To come to Him is never to be hungry
again, and never to be thirsty, for He is the
living water, the bread of life, the living
Jesus. He can only give Himself totally.
The idea of His 'cup overflowing' could
suggest that His giving to us is so generous
that it is overflowing and there's no
possibility of getting any more in!

In other words, He gives His all to us and
more. "What more could I have done for
you?" Jesus asks. *(cf. Good Friday Liturgy)*

The significance of the 'cup' is beautifully portrayed by my friend in the following writing:–

The Cup
A cup is a cup you may say.
You've every right: they all have the same function – that lips will touch and contents taken.

Reach out now and take a cup.
Any old one. Or a very special or treasured or valuable one.
Look at it.   Its colour, shape, size. It could be with or without handle.
Is it more mundane or more aesthetic?
Usually the more aesthetic an object becomes, the more stylized it becomes, and ends up by being almost or totally non functional.
A cup is a cup you may say.
However pretty, valuable, ornate, deco-rated, stylised - you can still drink from it.

Feel it.
Close your eyes now. The better to feel it.
Let you hands cup it, your fingers explore it, running over every part: inside, outside.
Let your finger and thumb explore the handle. Your feel will tell you about its quality.

Think of **how it has been used.**
A cup is a cup you may say. Both king and pauper slake their thirst at its edges. Both dull and intelligent drain its contents. Both sinner and saint, infant and nonagenarian, black and white. The cup is used for all kinds of purposes. The cup holding the last drop for the condemned man: the cup being hurled in anger; the cup being shared by two in love: the cup being offered to a stranger. A cup is a cup you may say.

But think of the Cup that He took.
He blessed it. He gave thanks for it. He gave it to his disciples. A cup is only a cup. What was that special one like? Where is that cup now? Was it ever used again? Does it really matter?
A cup is a cup you may say.

The cup may change, but on the altar the contents are always the same. He still blesses it, and gives Himself to us, again and again.

A cup is a cup you may say.

But for a while my body is the inadequate vessel that holds this precious Lord.

In the early Church, the Eucharist was called the 'breaking of bread'. We're told in the Acts of the Apostles: "The early Christian community remained faithful to the teaching of the apostles, to the brotherhood, to the 'breaking of bread' and to the prayers." *(Acts 2:42)*

The Eucharist was and still is after all these years, the centre of the Catholic Church's Life. It is the meal, the banquet for those who are hungry.
Through it, Christ is received in 'Person', as the living bread come down from heaven. *(John 6:51)* With Him, we receive the pledge of eternal life and the foretaste of the eternal banquet of the heavenly Jerusalem.

Christ Jesus becomes present in the Eucharist, whole and entire, in the reality of His body and blood, at every Mass, where His Glory remains veiled in mystery.

"I remained in the midst of my apostles in the Eucharist, in the heart of my holy Mother" he said. "Could I have deserted My poor children completely? You, my child, seek Me always in the Eucharist. It is for everyone...

Consider the height, the greatness of the gift, the depth of God Himself, the breadth, the gift for everyone in My Eucharist and bring others to it."
('He and I', Gabrielle Bossis, p.167)

The Eucharist is the Bread of Life, the 'daily bread' that sustains millions of Catholics throughout the world. St. John Chrysostom wrote, "In Holy Communion, God comes to us in a bodily way; our mouths touch the Body of Our Lord, as Our Lady's lips did."

Listen to Jesus' words in St. John's Gospel. "Anyone who eats My flesh and drinks My blood has eternal life. I shall raise him up on the last day." (John 6:54)

"He who eats My flesh and drinks My blood, lives in Me and I live in him." (John 6:56-57)

"I tell you solemnly, 'If you do not eat of the flesh of the Son of man and drink of His blood, you will not have life in you." (John 6:53)

Hearing these words the Jews remonstrated with one another, "How can this man give us His flesh to eat?", but that is exactly

221

what Jesus said he would do. *(John 6:52)*
Many of His followers couldn't take what
Jesus was saying:
"This is intolerable language," they said,
"How could anyone accept it?" *(John 6:60)*

And, of course, on a human level, one
cannot accept or understand. Only God's
incredible gift of faith can enable! The
words that follow make me so sad.

"After this, many of His disciples left Him
and stopped going with Him." *(John 6:64)*

Of course Jesus meant what He said. He
was well aware of what was going on in
people's hearts and minds, since He can
read hearts. He was aware too of His
followers complaining, and how they were
reacting to His words: "Stop complaining to
each other." *(John 6:64)*
Previously, knowing full well what was in
their hearts, He had asked: "Does this
upset you?" *(John 6:61)*

"Jesus knew from the outset those who did
not believe, and who it was who would
betray Him." *(John 6:64)*
He gives us our free will to respond to Him
or not. No one can believe for you. This is

the most wonderful thing about human beings. We can choose for ourselves. We must respond to God's call ourselves. If we choose God, we cannot do better. We will always get back an overflowing measure.

Jesus went on to say: "This is why I told you, that no one could come to Me, unless the Father allows him." *(John 6:65)*
Every call is grace, never forget.
Such a gift! Such a mystery of our faith!
Such a privilege to be called and chosen, to eat at this banquet!
"How can I repay the Lord for his goodness to me?, the cup of salvation I will take up."
(Psalm 116:12)

Just imagine what the Good Shepherd has done for us:
"You have prepared a banquet for me in the sight of my foes, my head you have anointed with oil, my cup is overflowing."
(Psalm 23:5)

This verse leaves me a bit speechless. On the one hand I see it full of mystery and heavenliness and on the other, I hear an echo of future sorrow for Jesus. It calls for deep faith and a humility to recognise our unworthiness, our helplessness, and our nothingness, in the face of the Almighty. "Let us bow and bend low, let us kneel before the God who made us, for we are the people He pastures, the flock that is led by His hand." *(Psalm 95:6-7)*

"Let all mortal flesh keep silence, and in fear and trembling stand..."

The Eucharist is the fullness of the gift of faith. It is the pearl hidden in the mystery of Scripture, the treasure hidden in the field of the Word of God, the secret of the Good Shepherd.

"In the Eucharist, God becomes present beside me on my path, in my knapsack, in friendship, close to my heart as a man." *(Carlo Carretto, 'In Search of the Beyond', p.99)*

The Eucharist is like the cloud which accompanied the People of God on their desert journey. In Old Testament times the manna, too, was a symbol of the Eucharist. This was the bread which fell miraculously from Heaven, fresh each day, to feed the Israelites in the desert. It is also like the pillar of fire, which pointed out the way through the depth of night, and so the night became clear as the day. *(cf. Exodus 16)*

The Eucharist is the 'heart beat' of the Catholic Faith. It is the Presence of Jesus among us, as the 'life blood' of the Church. There is no Church without Eucharist. "This is My Body given (broken) for you, this is My Blood poured out for you". *(Luke 22:19-20)*

His Body and Blood flow through our bloodstream, as we become new creations, when we receive the Eucharist. In this sacrament Jesus carries all our brokenness and takes it into Himself.

"The Holy Eucharist is Jesus... All Jesus!... In the Eucharist, You are there my beloved Jesus, living and whole, as fully as You were in the holy house of Nazareth. Oh, let me never leave the Presence of the Holy Eucharist for a single minute, as long as Jesus allows me to be there."
('Silent Pilgrimage to God', Charles de Foucauld, p.33)

In this faith of his in the Eucharist, Charles de Foucauld is no more mistaken than the Curé d'Ars, who in tears at the Altar, clasped the consecrated host and said, 'Jesus, if I knew I was not going to see You in Heaven, I should never let You go now.'

"The Eucharist is Jesus present on our altars, always, yes, to the end of time, the true Emmanuel! 'God with us', at all times, and everywhere on earth, exposed to our gaze, our adoration and our love, and by means of this perpetual Presence transforming the nights of our lives into a lustrous splendour".

(Charles de Foucauld - L'Evangile présenté aux Pauvres du Sahara, Arthaud, Paris 1937, 21st talk, p.145.)

For Charles de Foucauld then, the Eucharist is so real a presence of Jesus in the tabernacle, that it brightens the whole land and becomes a source of sanctification and salvation for all the people round it.

Catholics believe that Jesus is truly present in the Eucharist, in the Tabernacle and at every Mass. Many saints have become saints through their absolute faith in Jesus' Presence in the Eucharist, spending long hours adoring Him and interceding for the whole world.

Some orders of religious have been set up in the past, for the sole purpose of perpetual adoration of the Blessed Sacrament, like the Reparation nuns in Limerick.

How we loved to go there as children and

just to be with the host, fascinated by the many glowing candles that adorned the altar, as we sat there wrapped in silence and enveloped in the peace. It was a big treat for us to get to the Reparation Convent for adoration. It had an 'other-worldliness' about it!

Some individuals have even lived on nothing else but the Eucharist, a rare grace from our Good Shepherd. I have a friend in London, who at this moment, also lives on nothing else but the Eucharist, for the past six years now! God alone suffices.

We cannot consider the Eucharist without reference to Jesus' beloved Mother. Mary's life incarnated the meaning of the Eucharist. The Eucharistic Bread which we receive, is the spotless flesh of her Son, Jesus. The Eucharist is the source and summit of Mary's Life. She will help us to understand the Eucharist better, if we ask her. If only we knew how much she loves us!

The core of the Catholic Faith is the Mass and the Eucharist. In the Holy Sacrifice of the Mass, the 'immolated' Jesus offers Himself as a Sacrifice to His Father in Heaven. We add our offering with Him.

What a sacred vocation Jesus has given to his anointed priests, to share in His Priesthood in such a profound way, to make Him present on our Altars! Without our priests, there would be no Mass and without Mass there would be no Eucharist.

We must respect our priests as God's specially anointed ministers and pray for them. They are specially called and chosen. I can still hear my own mother saying; "Never criticise a priest, they are God's 'specially' anointed." How true! Lord we ask forgiveness for any negative word we may have ever said against your priests. Please bless each one of your chosen shepherds.

During each Mass, the bread and wine are changed into the Body and Blood of Jesus Christ, through the sacred ministry of the priest, by the power of the Holy Spirit. Some use the word 'transubstantiation', which means one substance (the bread and wine) being changed completely into another substance (the Body and Blood of Jesus). This gift was given to the Apostles at the Last Supper, where the Eucharist and the Priesthood were born. Jesus is the High Priest, par excellence.

"You are a priest of the order of
Melchizedek, and forever *(Psalm 110:4)*

The Power of Priesthood was first vested by
Jesus in Saint Peter, one of His apostles,
when He told Peter, He would build His
Church upon him, the Rock. Every priest,
since then, in the Catholic Church, traces
his priesthood back to St. Peter. It is a
direct line. Hence the sacredness of the
priesthood, commemorated each year on
Maundy Thursday as the priests of each
diocese gather round their bishop.

The setting for the institution of the
Eucharist was the Jewish Passover Meal,
which Jesus longed to celebrate with His
twelve Apostles the night before he died.
They were gathered in the Upper Room in
Jerusalem at Jesus' request.

Though the apostles did not realise it at the
time this was to be His last meal with them
before His Passion and Death. They could
see that Jesus heart was heavy for some
reason. "He was troubled in spirit," we are
told in John's Gospel. *(13:21)*

Later they were to discover that Judas
Iscariot, one of the twelve, who was at table

with them, was on the verge of betraying
Jesus his Friend and Master, to the chief
priests for thirty pieces of silver.

The Apostles were upset also as they heard
Jesus say that one of them would betray
Him. They were wondering who it was.
Such sadness mingled with joy! Jesus
identified the traitor for them, as the one to
whom He would give the bread dipped in
the dish. "As soon as Judas Iscariot had
taken the piece of bread, he went out.
Night had fallen" *(John 13:30)* The devil had
entered into him. *(John 13:27)*

The Darkness of sin was emerging to try to
defeat the Light. Judas betrayed Jesus'
friendship, and sold Him for thirty pieces of
silver.
A terrible moment! Jesus' hour had come!
His Passion was to begin. The 'Hour' He
dreaded. The 'Cup' of Suffering which He
saw at the time of His prayer in the Garden
of Gethsemane, with Peter, James and
John, was overflowing now and was about
to become a reality.

This Passover meal, which Jesus had
looked forward to so much, and longed for
with all His heart, was the start of a hard

and lonely road for Him, the way of intense suffering. Yet His beautiful heart was always thinking how best He could leave His Presence with His apostles when He had gone, in spite of His own sorrow, and so he instituted the Eucharist.

His command: "Do this in memory of Me," He said at His Last Supper." *(Luke 22:19)* "Take this and share it among you, because from now on, I tell you, I shall not drink wine until the Kingdom of God comes.

Then he took some bread, and when He had given thanks, He broke it and gave it to them, saying: 'This is My Body, which will be given for you: Do this as a memorial of Me'. He did the same after supper, and said: 'This cup is the new Covenant in My blood, which will be poured out for you.'" *(Luke 22: 17-20)*

The Eucharistic meal has a profoundly and primarily sacrificial meaning to us. Christ makes the sacrifice offered once for all on Calvary, present to us anew, as we remember at every Mass, the marks of His Passion and Death. We are reminded too, that the Risen Jesus will come again in glory at the end of time, at the end of history, and only the Father knows the moment of His coming.

"Seek Me always in the Eucharist. It is there for you, for everyone. Don't be reticent, come simply, give thanks with joy in your heart. Love simply. Everything is so simple with Me. Don't you notice this when I speak to you. Leave behind your old way of imagining. Enter into the way of love's clear vision. *(Charles de Foucauld: 'Silent Pilgrimage to God, p.167)*

The Eucharist must always be linked with love. St. Paul reminds us clearly in 1 Corinthians: 13:1-8 that one could not imagine a Eucharistic Celebration which lacked charity or care for the poor!

"In the Host, My heart is beating as it did on earth, as it does in Heaven. There are not many hearts of Christ. There is only one. Believe without the shadow of doubt, in My Presence, here before you and comfort Me by bringing your heart close to Mine. Look how alone I am in the empty Church. I knew it would be like this and yet, I instituted My Eucharist. I would feed even a single soul with the host.

Speak with the Host, as with your
most gentle and intimate friend.
The Host is listening to you and
you may be sure that you are
most dearly loved. Breathe freely.
Relax. Leave the earth. Enter the
realm of the Spirit. Let yourself
be carried away. Do you want to
come? Tell me about your
impatience to join Me. You are
Mine. How could you keep
yourself to yourself?"
('He and I', Gabrielle Bossis, p.119)

Pope John Paul II wrote very encouragingly:
"The Presence of Jesus in the tabernacle,
must be a kind of magnetic pull, attracting
an ever greater number of souls enamoured
of Him, ready to wait patiently to hear His
voice, and as it were, to sense the beating
of His heart. 'O, taste and see that the
Lord is sweet.' *(Psalm 34:8)*

Let us take the time to kneel before Jesus
present in the Eucharist, in order to make
reparation by our faith and love, for the acts
of carelessness and neglect, and even the
insults which our Saviour must endure, in
many parts of the world."
(John Paul II, 'Abide with us Lord' p.18)

"Stay with us, for it is almost evening", was the invitation to the traveller, from the two disciples on the road to Emmaus. As He came up and walked beside them, their hearts were heavy with sadness after the disastrous events in Jerusalem. Their best Friend and Master Jesus, had just been brutally crucified, had died and was buried, and all they could think of was of Him. They certainly did not expect to find Him alive.

Little did they know that He was the stranger walking beside them, except, as they spoke of Him, and to Him, their hearts burned within them with great love. Something was different, special, about this traveller who was intending to go on further.

What a revelation for them, when He accepted their invitation to stay with them! "Now while He was at table with them, He took the bread and said the blessing; then He broke the bread and handed it to them." *(Luke 24:30)*
They recognized Him in the 'breaking of bread', the Eucharist. "And their eyes were opened, but He had vanished from their sight." *(Luke 24:31)* He had revealed to them

on the way, that everything written about
Him in the Prophets and Psalms, was
fulfilled in Him.

After that experience they could never be
the same again. What transformation
happened in their lives having met Him,
having shared the Eucharist with Him. To
know that He is alive! What privilege! "Stay
with us Lord, for it is almost evening and
the day is far spent" they had said. It is our
prayer and invitation too.

"When minds are enlightened and hearts
are enkindled, signs begin to "speak". The
Eucharist unfolds in a dynamic context of
signs, containing a rich and luminous
message. Through these signs, the mystery
in some way opens up before the eyes of
the believer".
(Pope John Paul II, 'Abide with us Lord', p.14)

It was through the Eucharist that Jesus
found a way to stay with the disciples
forever. Receiving the Eucharist means
entering into the most profound
communion with Him.

"Abide with Me and I in you," Jesus says.
(John 15:4) He wants us to be close to Him

as our Friend. He wants us to be at His side, so that we can fill our hearts with the experience of His friendship, which alone gives meaning and fulfilment to our lives.

Try, with God's help, to love the Eucharist more and more. Try, too, if you are busy, to treat yourself if you can, to Holy Mass a few times a week, or even a visit to the Blessed Sacrament. I pray we will all become more and more aware of the power and wonder of the Eucharist.

"The Eucharist, not only provides the inner strength needed for our mission for the Good Shepherd, but it is also in some sense its 'plan'. For the Eucharist is a mode of being, which passes from Jesus into each Christian, through whose testimony it is meant to spread throughout society and culture. For this to happen, each member of the faithful must assimilate, through personal and communal meditation, the values which the Eucharist expresses, the attitudes it inspires, the resolutions to which it gives rise." ('Abide with us Lord', Pope John Paul II, p.25)

I suggest you treat yourself to a copy of this lovely pamphlet produced by C.T.S. called

'Abide with us Lord' by our late Pope John Paul II. It is lovely, easily read, and well worthwhile.

"The Eucharist makes the risen Christ constantly present; Christ who continues to give Himself to us, calling us to participate in the banquet of His Body and His Blood. From this full communion with Him comes every other element of the life of the Church, in the first place the communion among the faithful, the commitment to proclaim and give witness to the Gospel, the ardour of charity towards all, especially towards the poor and the smallest."
('Give yourself to Christ', Pope Benedict XVI, 20th April 2005: C.T.S. Pamphlet)

"I need bread, but I assure you I feel the need of friendship quite as much, and nothing gives me the friendship of Jesus more than the Gospel and the Eucharist.
You will tell me I am old-fashioned to go on believing in visits to the Blessed Sacrament. Still, I do believe that Jesus is present in the Eucharist not only during the Mass, but also between one Mass and the next, always. And how helpful this belief has been to me; what great things this Presence has given me!"
(Carlo Carretto: 'In Search of the Beyond', p.100)

As you will no doubt have noticed, I love
the spirituality of Carlo Carretto so much
and it has been an inspiring part of my
spiritual growth for many years now. I
would love to share with you this beautiful
spiritual experience Our Lord gave Him, in
relation to the Eucharist. His life would
have been so empty without it. Of course
the Good Shepherd knew how special his
love for the Eucharist was, and so He gave
him this choicest grace.

On his journey towards the Lord, Carlo
became completely worn out, and he felt he
just couldn't go another step. All that was
before him was his past, his sins, his errors.
He was desperate to find joy and peace.

As always the Good Shepherd is around
keeping close watch over His sheep, and
listening to their greatest need. He came to
Carlo in a way he never expected.

> "Jesus," he explained, "became
> a Sacrament for me, the cause
> of my salvation. He brought my
> time in hell to an end, and put a
> stop to my inner disintegration.
> He washed me patiently in the
> waters of Baptism, He filled me

with the exhilarating joy of the
Holy Spirit in Confirmation. He
nourished me with the bread of
His Word. Above all, He
forgave me, He forgot
everything; He did not even
wish me to remember my past
myself.

When, through my tears, I
began to tell Him something of
the years during which I
betrayed Him, He lovingly
placed His hand on my mouth in
order to silence me. His one
concern was that I should
muster courage enough to pick
myself up again, to try and carry
on walking in spite of my
weakness, and to believe in His
love in spite of my fears.

But there was one thing He did,
the value of which cannot be
measured, something truly
unbelievable, something only
God could do.

While I continued to have doubts
about my own salvation, to tell
Him that my sins could not be
forgiven, and that justice, too,

had its rights, He appeared on
the Cross before me one Friday
towards midday.
I was at its foot, and found
myself bathed with the blood
which flowed from the gaping
holes made in His flesh by the
nails. He remained there for
three hours until He expired.

I realized that He had died in
order that I might stop turning
to Him with questions about
justice, and believe instead, deep
within myself, that the scales
had come down overflowing on
the side of love, and that even
though all men through unbelief
or madness had offended Him,
He had conquered forever, and
drawn all things everlastingly to
Himself.

Then later, so that I should
never forget that Friday and
abandon the Cross, as one
forgets a postcard on a table,
or a picture in a worn out book
that had been feeding ones
devotion, He led me on to

discover that in order to be with me continually, not simply as an affectionate remembrance but as a living presence, He had devised the Eucharist.

What a discovery that was! Under the sacramental sign of bread, Jesus was there each morning to renew the sacrifice of the Cross and make of it, the living sacrifice of His bride, the Church, a pure offering to the Divine Majesty.
And still that was not all.
He led me on to understand that the sign of bread testified to His hidden Presence, not only during the Great Sacrifice, but at all times, since the Eucharist was not an isolated moment in my day, but a line which stretched over twenty- four hours: He is God-with-us, the realisation of what had been foretold by the 'cloud' that went before the people of God during their journey through the desert, and the 'darkness' which filled the tabernacle in the temple at Jerusalem.

I must emphasize that this vital
realization that the sign of bread
concealed and pointed out for
me the uninterrupted Presence
of Jesus beside me, was a
unique grace in my life. From
that moment He led me along
the path to intimacy, and
friendship with Himself. I
understood that He longed to be
present like this beside each one
of you. Jesus was not only
bread, He was also a Friend."
*('In Search of the Beyond', Carlo
Carretto, p.58-60)*

So our wonderful Good Shepherd simply
thinks of everything, and cares like no one
else could, for His precious sheep. He
never leaves a stone unturned if He can
help us. This Banquet of the Eucharist,
where his Presence is veiled, is nothing
compared to the Banquet He has prepared
for us in Heaven, where there will be no
more sorrow.

Before I close this chapter on the Eucharist,
I would like to share with you a most
wonderful Scripture passage where Jesus is
prophetically leading us to understand the

Mystery, through His compassionate love and care for the multitude that followed Him.

Imagine yourself to be there... ... You might imagine you are one of the crowd... you may be one of the children... you may be tired and weary and be in need of rest... you may be hungry and be in need of food... you may be suffering from sickness of one kind or another and be in need of healing, hoping Jesus will touch you... or you may be there because your friends were going and they asked you to come along... or you may be just plain curious.

You might be one of the distributors of the bread, or you may be a collector of what is left over, you may have brought something to Jesus for Him to transform for you or you may even be one of the apostles, devoting your whole life to His service. However you come, and for whatever reason, simply imagine you are there. Jesus sees you there. He has just received the news that John the Baptist has been beheaded by Herod. Remember John the Baptist was Jesus' cousin, and it was the same John who prepared the way for Jesus, calling people to repentance in preparation for Jesus coming, so it looks as if John's work was done.

"When Jesus received this news, He withdrew by boat to a lonely place where they could be by themselves. But the people heard of this and, leaving the towns, went after Him on foot. So as He stepped ashore, He saw a large crowd; and He took pity on them and healed the sick.

When evening came, the disciples went to Him and said, 'This is a lonely place, and the time has slipped by; so send the people away, and they can go to the village and buy themselves food.' Jesus replied, 'There is no need for them to go: give them something to eat yourselves'.
But they answered, 'All we have with us is five loaves and two fish.' 'Bring them here to me,' He said.

He gave orders that the people were to sit down on the grass; then He took the five loaves and two fish, and raised His eyes to Heaven and said the blessing. And breaking the loaves He handed them to His disciples who gave them to the crowds. They all ate as much as they wanted, and they collected the scraps remaining, twelve baskets full. Those who ate numbered about five thousand men, to say nothing of women and children." *(Matthew 14:13-21)*

Today it is not just five thousand Jesus feeds, it is millions all over the world, whom He feeds and nourishes with the Eucharist. It is food for those who are called and chosen and who respond with a heart of love. "As often as you eat this bread and drink this cup, you proclaim the Lord's death until He comes." *(1 Corinthians 11:26)* What a Gift!

Prayer of St. Damascene

O God, my God,
You are a consuming and invisible fire.
Because of Your great love,
You gave me Your Body as food and
made me worthy to share in Your Divinity.
Permeate my whole body and soul,
all my limbs and faculties;
Burn up all my wickedness;
Enlighten my soul;
Give understanding to my mind;
Sanctify my body

Make me a dwelling
place for You,
together with Your blessed Father
and all-Holy Spirit,
that I may also be in You always,
through the prayers of
Your most pure Mother,
and all the saints. Amen
(late 7th-mid 8th C.)

PRAYER FOR PRIESTS

Lord Jesus,
You have chosen Your priests from among
us and sent them out to proclaim Your
Word, to act in Your name.
For so great a gift to your Church, we give
you praise and thanksgiving.

Inspire them through prayer to live each
day the mystery of your dying and rising.
Make them constant in prayer for poor
sinners. May the Holy Spirit put Your word
on their lips and Your love in their hearts,
to bring good news to the poor and healing
to the broken-hearted.

And may the gift of Mary Your mother, to the disciple whom He loved, be Your gift to every priest. Grant that she who formed You in her human image, may form them in Your divine image, by the power of Your Spirit, to the glory of God the Father. Amen.

Let us pray God's blessing upon all our priests, expecially those I name here: … …

… … … … … … …   … … …

Heavenly Father, send Your blessing upon these chosen ones. Fill them with the fire of Your love, that their ministry may reveal Your presence in the Church.

May Your power shine out through their weakness, since they are earthen vessels. In their affliction let them never be crushed; in their doubts never despair; in temptation never be destroyed; in persecution never abandoned.

In times of weakness send them Your Spirit, and help them always to praise You now and forever. Amen.

A Favourite Prayer of Mine:

Soul of My Saviour, sanctify my breast;
Body of Christ, be Thou my saving guest;
Blood of My Saviour, bathe me in Thy tide,
Wash me in water flowing from Thy side.

Strength and protection may Thy Passion be;
O blessèd Jesus hear and answer me;
Deep in Thy wounds, Lord,
hide and shelter me;
So shall I never, never part from Thee.

Guard and defend me from the foe malign;
In death's dread moments make me only Thine;
Call me, and bid me come to Thee on high,
When I may praise Thee with Thy saints for
aye.
(Ascribed to John XXII 1249-1334; tr. Anonymous)

And by the way, did you know that the Lord our God is a God of Bounty, He can only give His total self to you.

His giving is super-abundant, "a full measure, pressed down, shaken together and running over, will be poured into your lap." *(Luke 6:38)*

"At-one with the All and so at-one with all; our True self-expresson – the expression of Himself through us."
('He and I', p.155)

Psalm Twenty Three

CHAPTER SEVEN

Surely Goodness and Kindness shall follow me all the days of my life. In the Lord's own house shall I dwell forever.
(Psalm 23:6)

GOODNESS WILL FOLLOW ME!

Lord, You are the Good Shepherd,
And I will follow You.
Now I have everything, because You provide
everything I need.
You watch over me
While I rest in the peaceful meadow of prayer,
And by the healing waters of my Baptism,
You give life to my soul.

You guard all my choices through the world,
Guiding me until I'm all and only for You,
And where there's love there's no fear
Until even my fear of death dissolves in Your
love
Because the Shepherd's love
Protects me from evil.

Sometimes, Lord, when I wander away,
You seek me out,
But punishment never comes after me.
You only look for me
Enfolding me
Correcting and forgiving me in love.

You choose me as Your guest.
You honour me and sit me down to
eat with You,
And never outdone in generosity,
Lavish as the most attentive Host,
Anointing me with the very gift of
Yourself
You nourish me with the Bread of
Life.

That's why, Lord, I have everything I
need,
I thank You that there's nothing else I
need.
If I stay close, You promise me life to
the full,
So I will follow You, Lord – The
Good Shepherd.
Secure in faith that I will one day
share Your life
With You for all Eternity.

(© Stephen Wilson, September 2005)

PSALM TWENTY THREE

The word 'follow' in Hebrew, actually means 'pursue'. Isn't that fantastic! David is saying that God's goodness will 'chase after him', like the hound of heaven, to the end of his days. Makes it sound as though there's no escape from God's Love! And sure there isn't! How wonderful! God is always awake! Should we lose sight of the Shepherd's goodness and love for us, when we get a bit mixed up, we can, when we're ready, do a turn around, only to find, He is still there pursuing us. What a promise!

What a psalm! What a God, whose Goodness is eternal. Makes me think of the need for us to be more alert, to 'stay awake'

and not get too drowsy in our following our
Good Shepherd. How comforting for us
wayward sheep that His goodness and His
mercy pursues us always!

I can't imagine living without God, without
faith, without my Church community,
without God's goodness all around me.
This is the Good Shepherd's promise. I feel
so showered with blessings, because God is
so good to me all the time, while others
seem to have such sorrow, sickness, and
even disaster, leading them to troubles and
sometimes despair. Some suffer and have a
serenity in their suffering that can only be a
special grace from the Good Shepherd.

However, I too can share with those less
fortunate some of the goodness God shares
with me, by doing my best for them when
He puts them in my path, or by carrying
them in my heart to Him often in prayer,
even though I don't know them at all,
begging Him to send them the 'right'
people for their need, at the 'right' time.
Some may be people I see on the street to
whom I may never speak. Do you ever
pray for people you just 'bump into' by the
way, when you notice a sad face or some
struggle 'on their face', or you see a deep

unhappiness or even bitterness in someone's heart? Do you ever just thank God for people's happiness when you see them rejoicing? Lest 'they' forget to thank Him, 'you' can do it for them, for you know that all good gifts come from Him. They might forget this or they may even never know it, and they'll never know you prayed for them, till later on in Heaven!

You may never meet again on earth but your awareness of them, and your bringing them to the Good Shepherd, has comforted *Him* greatly, and blessed the ground where you have trod and hopefully blest them too. I do this often! Do you? He always knows the 'right time' for each sheep, doesn't He? Well, that's my experience anyway, and that's how I live. You have no time then for self centredness or self pity and you don't waste the precious moments God gives you each day on 'waste of time' thoughts! Every day becomes filled with worthwhile-ness! Sometimes living 'in awareness' will mean asking help from good friends here and there, who can help in 'your stead.'

To have 'real' Christian friends is just another sign of His goodness, and is such a bonus, isn't it? Just what would we do without these great friends? We'd be lost without them. It's all part of the showering of His goodness, part of being his family. We are His flock and we do belong together no matter what.

And when I think of kindness, I think of giving without counting the cost. If you do count the cost, you've lost it! Kindness is a beautiful fruit of the Holy Spirit, it's part of God's abundance, of His sensitive, discreet, gentle but lavish giving. To be at the receiving end of beautiful kindness sometimes, is simply breath taking, and leaves one speechless. It's going the 'extra' mile... as Jesus teaches us. *(Matthew 5:42)* I am totally overwhelmed on occasion by people's kindness. Some people are kindness personified but unfortunately, there are far too few of these.

My friend Kathy Straughan read this little poem to me on the phone the other day, as we talked of the Lord's goodness to us. She doesn't know who wrote it, but I thought you may find it helpful, as I do.

The way to really live:
To be glad of life because it gives you a chance

To love and to work and to play
and to look at the stars.
To be satisfied with your possessions
but not content with yourself
until you have made the best use of them.
To despise nothing in the world
except what is false and mean.
To fear nothing except what is cowardly.
To be guided by what you admire and love
rather than by what you hate.
To envy nothing that is your neighbour's
except his kindness of heart
and gentleness of manner.
To think seldom of your enemies
often of your friends
and everyday of Christ.
(Anonymous - and cf. Philippians 4:8)

Others have to struggle for faith and I
didn't, because of my wonderful parents,
who brought me to the faith as a baby, and
had me baptized, so that I grew up with the
faith. No thanks to me! There can be no
deserving of it, only a truly grateful heart for
so many blessings received as a result of it,
and of growing up in an Irish catholic
family. One of the most wonderful signs of
God's goodness must surely be the creation
of family. As human beings we all need to
belong, to have roots; to be accepted for

who we are, with all our individual
differences and talents. We all need a place
we can call 'home'. There is in each of us,
a deep instinctive need to belong, to love,
and to be loved. Love must always be self-
diffusive. Love has a need to give itself
away. As the prophet Khalil Gibran says:
"It's when you give of yourself that you truly
give." It starts with parents' love for each
other, then their love for the children, then
the childrens' love for each other, then their
love flowing outwards to the whole human
family. Love of its nature must always be
given away. It is the same with goodness,
it cannot be stored away. It must be freely
given.

So to share His goodness and love with
unbelievers, or with those who struggle with
the faith, or with those who've strayed from
the faith for whatever reason, I simply pray
for them, that they too, will receive this
great gift of faith and cherish it, or that they
will return home to the Good Shepherd.
There are so many people who only in the
next world will know who prayed for them!
You can pray you know for them, at any
place and at any time, when you are stuck
in a traffic jam, as I'm sure all those people
on the roads with you, don't know their

Good Shepherd as you do. Perhaps they have been let down or perhaps they haven't had the chance yet! You can ask the Good Shepherd to 'hurry up' with them. I often wonder where everyone is going and I end up telling the Lord how wonderful He is, because He is the only One who knows everyone, who knows where everyone is going, and He is the only way!

I'm reminded of the words in Scripture: "When a man has a great deal given him, a great deal will be demanded of him; when a man has a great deal given to him in trust, even more will be expected of him." *(Luke 12: 48)* So I ask you to pray for me to honour what God has done for me so generously. In my life, the Lord has shown me a super abundance of goodness and kindness and I have everything to thank Him for daily. It's imperative I learn to share! We learn from the parable of the talents, that everything we have is for sharing. An excellent way of spreading God's goodness is to share it.

God Himself loved us so much, that having created us, He wanted to share everything with us, even more so after our first parent's fall from grace. He shares His creation with us, but more than that, He shares Himself, His goodness, His life, His happiness, His home, His only Son. He did not create to get but to give, for we can give Him nothing. We're always at the receiving end of God's goodness. "Of His fullness we have all received." *(Prologue of St. John 1:16)*

I love the priestly blessing in the book of Numbers and you can wish it on your family and friends and even your enemies if any!
"May the Lord bless you and keep you.
May He let His face shine on you and be gracious to you.
May the Lord uncover His face to you and bring you peace.
This is how they are to call down My name on the Sons of Israel,
and I will bless them." *(Numbers 6:23-27)*

To wish goodness and kindness to pursue someone all the days of their life is a most gracious blessing. We are so blest to have our Church family of love, enabling God's friends to dwell in the house of the Lord all the days of their life. We see in the Acts of the Apostles how important community was for the growth of the early Church, and how the Lord on many

occasions showed His goodness to the
Apostles by working miracles through them;
(Acts 19:11) by sending the Holy Spirit upon
those for whom they prayed; *(Acts 10:44-48)*
by many miracles and conversions; by
adding several thousands to their numbers.
"That very day 3,000 were added to the
their numbers." *(Acts 2:41)* Fairly soon,
there were thousands more added, and so
the Church began.

The life of Jesus flows through us, and
beyond us to others, circulating to all parts
of His Body the Church, in all parts of the
world. The Holy Spirit has empowered the
Church with gifts. We see the diversity of
these gifts used for the building up of His
Kingdom. What magnificent work we can
do together for Him.

Our beautiful and 'miraculous' Bosnian
project, *(9 miles from Medugorje),* through
working together for Him since 1992, has
blossomed into providing healing and new life
for our refugees, thanks to our benefactors.
Of His goodness, He has provided homes for
them, with gardens, vegetables, flowers, pigs,
chickens, everything beyond their dreams,
and even now a beautiful new church and
chapel, where they can more easily enjoy

Him! To Him be praise and glory! We only
need a vineyard! *(Isaiah 5:1)*
We are privileged to be workers in the family,
God's family. Jesus is our God- connection.

> "You water the land and care for it,
> Enriching it with natural resources.
> God's stream is filled with water;
> So You prepare the earth
> To give us its fruits.
> You drench the furrows in the land
> And level the ridges,
> You soften the soil with showers
> And bless its crops.
> You crown the year with your
> goodness;
> Abundance flows everywhere.
> The deserts have become pasture land,
> The hills are clothed with gladness,
> The meadows covered with flocks,
> The valleys decked with grain –
> They shout and sing for joy."
> *(Psalm 65:9-14)*

The Catholic Church is alive today. The
more we are aware of the poor, the more
alive we become and the more we will
become God's Family. We all need each
other. "No man is an island," John Donne
rightly says.

St. Paul sums up the workings of the Church (the Communion of Faith) so brilliantly in the following analogy: "So then, the eye cannot say to the hand , "I don't need you!" Nor can the head say to the feet, "Well, I don't need you". On the contrary, we cannot do without the parts of the body that seem to be weaker; and those parts that we think aren't worth very much, are the ones which we treat with greater care; while the parts of the body which don't look very nice, are treated with special modesty, which the most beautiful parts do not need. God Himself has put the body together in such a way as to give greater honour to those parts that need it.

And so, there is no division in the body, but all its different parts have the same concern for one another. If one part of the body suffers, all the other parts suffer with it; if one part is praised, all the other parts share its happiness. All of you are Christ's body, and each one is a part of it. In the Church, God has put all in place." *(1 Corinthians 12:21-28, Good News Bible)*

Jesus chose St. Peter to feed His lambs and His sheep. Peter had previously denied Jesus, but he was heartily sorry for it.

"Aren't you one of this man's disciples?"
they asked Peter. "I am not," Peter
answered. Three times, Peter was asked
the same question. Part of God's Goodness
to us, is to be able to take each day as 'new'
and start again.

Later, Jesus gave Peter a huge chance, as
He does us. He asks Peter a very special
'personal' question, when He was with
some of the disciples after the Resurrection:
"Simon, son of John, do you love Me more
than these others do?" Peter answered,
"Yes, Lord, You know I love You." Jesus
said to him, "Feed My Lambs."
A second time Jesus said to Peter:
"Simon, son of John, do you love Me?"
Peter replied, "Yes, Lord, you know I love
You." Jesus said to him, "Look after my
sheep."
Then He said to him a third time: "Simon,
son of John, do you love Me?"
Peter was upset that Jesus asked him the
third time, "Do you love Me?" and said,
"Lord, You know everything; You know I
love You." Jesus said to him, "Feed My
sheep." *(John 21:15-17)*.

The goodness and kindness of God is always
being freely poured upon us. *(cf. Titus 3:4-7)*

Jesus is giving Peter a fresh chance to make up for his three denials, giving him a fresh opportunity to pour out his love, and to yield his life wholeheartedly for his sheep and lambs.

"If you love Me, feed My lambs and My sheep." *(John 21:16)*

It was the same Peter that Jesus asked who did men say He was. Spontaneously Peter replied: "You are the Christ, the Son of the living God!" Similarly, Martha used almost identical words. *(John 11:27)* Jesus must have been so delighted at Peter's response, congratulating him. "Simon, son of John," Jesus said, "You are a happy man! Because it was not flesh and blood that revealed this to you, but My Father in Heaven." *(Matthew 16:15-20)*

We hear many wonderful stories of the power of conversion of heart. Peter is no exception. He had let Jesus down very badly in public, at a vital time in Jesus' life, saying he did not know Him. In fact, at the time they were becoming very good friends.

We can see what a moment of panic and fear and weakness can do in our lives. We all know that fear can make a person behave 'out of character'. We're so vulnerable sometimes! But we know too, that Jesus' look of love and forgiveness changed Peter forever.

He had no intention of ever deserting His Master, or of letting Him down. It was a moment of sheer panic, under terrifying circumstances, and it was not really the 'true' Peter that shows. Paul too, writes about the things we do not want to do, saying that they are the very things we do in our weakness and this is exactly what happened to him, too:—

"The fact is that I know of nothing good living in me, living that is in my unspiritual self. For, though the will to do what is good is in me, the performance is not, with the result that instead of doing the good things I want to do, I carry out the sinful things I do not want. When I act against my will, then it is not my true self doing it, but sin lives in me.

In fact, this seems to be the rule, that every single time I want to do good, it is something evil that comes to hand. In my inmost self I dearly love God's Law, but I can see that my body follows a different law that battles against the law which my reason dictates. This is what makes me a prisoner of that law of sin, which lives inside my body". *(Romans 7:18-23)*

Don't we know this ourselves! Our many good friends in AA (that anointed spiritual programme for alcoholics) would know this very specially, too, as they struggle to overcome the evil of alcohol in their lives. Many, thank God, with great success.

Fortunately Jesus could see straight into Peter's heart, He knew it well. Jesus' look picked Peter up, gave him the chance he needed, and helped him to live again, to face his brothers again, to trust his life to the Good Shepherd again, with greater commitment than ever. May be it was a happy fault! How often does the worst thing that happens to us, turn out to be the best! (seen mostly in retrospect!)

Peter must have cried out with the psalmist: "What can I ever do for the Lord, in return for all He has done for me?"*(Psalm 116)* The joy of being forgiven, the peace of knowing that love was not withdrawn, the amazing response of love from Peter from now on, made him experience a beautiful 'metanoia', a change of outlook, which would heal him forever and which would

allow him to receive the Lord's Goodness and Kindness towards himself forever.
"There is no fear in love; perfect love casts out fear." *(1 John 4:18)* Dear Peter was able to accept forgiveness from Jesus, forgive himself, let go of his sin, start again, and spend the rest of his life and energy 'in the House of the Lord' making Jesus the Good Shepherd known everywhere he went. "In the Lords own house shall I dwell forever." *(Psalm 23:6)* Such a favour!

This would certainly have been Peter's dream fulfilled.
"Let me stay in your tent forever, taking refuge in the shelter of Your wings." *(Psalm 61:4)*
"The Lord is My Shepherd there is nothing I shall want, in the Lord's own house shall I dwell forever." *(Psalm 23:1,6)*
"Happy those who dwell in Your House forever and can praise You all day." *(Psalm 84:4)*

Poor Peter, he couldn't show enough love for Jesus after his moment of weakness. As the first Pope of the Church, he worked very hard to make Jesus known, having the privilege at the end of his life to die for his Master, but as Jesus had foretold of him,

"Another will lead you, where you would rather not go!" *(John 21:18)* However, Jesus knew that Peter had it in his heart to die for Him, because at the last supper, when Jesus said He was going away, Peter wanted to follow Him, declaring that he would go to prison with him and even die for Him. *(cf. John 13:36-38)*

"Directly after the feeding of the five thousand, Jesus made the disciples get into the boat and go on ahead to the other side while He would send the crowds away. After sending the crowds away, Jesus went up into the hills by Himself to pray. When evening came, He was there alone, while the boat, by now far out on the lake, was battling with a heavy sea, for there was a head wind.

In the fourth watch of the night He went towards them, walking on the lake, and when the disciples saw Him walking on the lake they were terrified. 'It is a ghost,' they said, and cried out in fear. But at once Jesus called out to them, saying, ' Courage! It is I! Do not be afraid'. It was Peter who answered. 'Lord,' he said, 'if it is You, tell me to come to You across the water.' 'Come' said Jesus. Then Peter got out of

the boat and started walking towards Jesus
across the water, but as soon as he felt the
force of the wind, he took fright and began
to sink. 'Lord! Save me!' he cried. Jesus
put out His hand at once and held Him.
'Man of little faith, why did you doubt?' And
as they got into the boat the wind dropped.
The men in the boat bowed down before
Him and said, 'Truly, You are the Son of
God.'" *(Matthew 14:22-33)*

Such love in Peter's heart for Jesus and
Jesus knew it! How Jesus was teaching
Him so powerfully. First Peter experienced
the miracle of the bread, (Eucharist) now he
experiences a huge struggle with head
winds and heavy seas, (symbolic of what he
might experience later as head of the
church), and Peter's need for courage in the
face of difficulties and the need to take risks
for the Gospel.

Then we have the beautiful assurance of
Jesus' Presence, at first disguised and then
real after Peter took the leap in faith and
stepped out of the boat, on to the water. Can
you imagine it? What a moment for dear
Peter ! Then we have Jesus' usual reassuring
words "Do not be afraid" *(A phrase used 366
times in Scripture, including 1 for leap year!)*

Amazing! What a scene! Peter was doing fine at first. The minute He looked at the problem (force of the wind) and not at Jesus, he started to sink!!! Are we not all the same?

We keep looking the wrong way at our problems and not at Jesus, the Solver of Problems. Is there a lesson for us here? Then, Jesus hearing Peter cry out 'Lord save me', put out His hand and held him. Another great moment for Peter being held by Jesus. How could he fear now? "Man of little faith, why did you doubt?" Jesus said to Peter. See yourself here also??

Next we're told: "As they got into the boat, the wind dropped." *(Matthew 14:22-33)* Jesus' Presence in the boat, with Peter back in it, brought the calm that was needed and we're told the wind dropped. The men in the boat bowed down before Him and said, "Truly, You are the Son of God." What a declaration of faith! What a beautiful friendship! Such love!

We too can truly bow down in adoration after we have experienced the power of Jesus carrying us through some problem or attack, or illness, and all we then can do, is to stare in amazement at the wonder of His Presence and adore. Perhaps to test our faith, He disguises himself sometimes, though we wish He wouldn't. Peter truly loved Jesus. We know that Peter was crucified upside down for love of his Jesus, his Shepherd King, his Lover and Best Friend, his Everything, unworthy as he said, to be crucified in the same manner as His Master.

Since Peter, there have been many martyrs and saints in the Catholic Church, some canonized and most not. Many today spend their energy and talents in the service of the Master, working under the umbrella of 'Church,' and spreading the Good News, that Jesus is alive today!

"They are happy who dwell in Your house Forever singing Your praise. They are happy whose hope is in You. In whose hearts are the roads to Zion". *(Psalm 84:4)*

One of our great successors of Saint Peter was our well beloved Pope, John Paul the Great, a man like Peter of contagious zeal for the Lord. As a tribute to him, I would like to include this wonderful photograph of him with Cardinal Wyszynski, taken in Rome on 23rd October 1978.

Pope John Paul II and Cardinal Wyszynski, 1978

This embrace speaks for itself. It conveys his immense love, warmth and goodness, and Fatherly love for his flock. In a special way, this picture symbolises the inseparable bond and solidarity between Peter and the Polish Church from which Pope John Paul II hailed. It may be thanks to Cardinal Wyszynski, that John Paul II was elected Pope. What an amazing witness he was for God! How He held the world captive for

Jesus Christ. I pray He will work more powerfully from Heaven to win many souls for the Good Shepherd.

"The love of Christ was the dominant force in the life of our former beloved Holy Father, Pope John Paul II. Anyone who ever saw him pray, who ever heard him preach, knows that. Thanks to his being profoundly rooted in Christ, He was able to bear a burden which transcends merely human abilities: that of being the Shepherd of Christ's Flock, His universal Church". *(Pope Benedict VI speaking at the funeral Mass of Pope John Paul II at the Vatican, Rome, 2005).*

Everything changes when we tell people what the Lord has done for us." Go and stand in the Temple and tell the people all about this new Life". *(Acts 5:20)* No one can fully convey the Good News of Jesus unless they have first experienced it for themselves. We see it with the apostles so clearly. The saying is 'Nemo dat quod non habet' – which translated means –'You can't give away what you haven't got'. You can only witness effectively to what you know. Personal experience and witness is best. I read somewhere recently that the world does not need a new Gospel. Jesus Christ is the Gospel. He has come in the flesh and is alive today. "I am the Resurrection and the Life," says Jesus, "if anyone believes in Me, though he dies, he will live, and whoever believes in Me, will never die." *(John 11:25-26)* We do not need a new Church today either, Christ's Church will go on till the end of time. Jesus promises that! "So I now say to you: 'You are Peter *(meaning 'rock')* and on this Rock *(meaning 'Peter')* I will build My Church and the gates of the underworld can never hold out against it. I will give you the keys of the kingdom; whatever you bind on earth shall be considered bound in heaven; whatever you loose on earth shall be considered loosed in heaven'." *(Matthew 16:18-20)*

What we do need is certainly more love, better evangelisation, more whole-hearted commitment to Jesus, and true witnesses. The true evangelist is not going to talk about Jesus, but he is going to witness to Jesus in the power of the Holy Spirit, telling people what Jesus means to him personally. Though there is always need for solid teaching, there is even more need today for witness. All who receive healing in Scripture, could witness to Him, to His goodness to them. Actions speak louder

than words, so the more we witness to
God's goodness and kindness and share it
with others, the better witnesses we will be.
More authentic! Meeting Jesus changes
lives forever !

Consumed by a burning fire, Carlo Carretto
writes:
"One thing, however, is certain:
Until we have accepted Him and borne
witness that He is the Son of God,
something will be missing from our life,
for us the sunlight will be mixed with
shadows, at dawn we will be filled with
nostalgia, and our nights will be restless. It
is inevitable!
If you ever have met anyone who has found
the answer to the mystery of life or peace
of heart without Jesus, come and tell me
about him, for I have never come across
such a one.
As for me, I began to know Jesus as soon
as I accepted Jesus as truth; I found true
peace when I actively sought His friendship;
and above all I experienced joy, true joy,
 that stands above the vicissitudes of life,
as soon as I tasted and experienced for
myself the gift He came to bestow on us:
eternal life".
(Carlo Carretto: 'In Search of the Beyond', p.57)

Each one has to discover Him for themselves. As the psalmist says: "I have learnt for myself that Yahweh is great." *(Psalm 135:5)*

Remember that incredible scene in St. John's Gospel, where Jesus talks to the Samaritan woman at the well. (Thereby breaking all the rules!) I love the way she became the first missionary in the world when she introduced the villagers to Jesus.

But in case she became too proud, thinking it was solely thanks to her efforts that they believed in Him, we read how they said: "Now we no longer believe because of what you told us; we have heard Him ourselves and we know that He really is the Saviour of the World." *(John 4:42)*
Isn't that something! All is grace!

To be a follower of Jesus, to know who He is and what He means, is to have a super abundance of life. When we live with Him, life becomes really worth living, and it seems to simplify, and we begin to 'live' in the real sense of the word.

"He is the New and Living Way". *(Hebrews 10:20)*

"The love of Christ overwhelms us when we reflect that if one man has died for all, then all men should be dead; and the reason He died for us all was so that living people should live no longer for themselves, but for Him who died and was raised to life for them… And for anyone who is in Christ there is a new creation; the old creation has gone, and now the new one is here."
(2 Corinthians 5:14-17)

"So few people live for Me and for others. Once in a while perhaps and then they turn to self-centredness. My child, let our two beings be so closely united, that the you in you is no longer noticed, and all your thoughts come homing to Me. I am your happiness. I created you this way, so that you might make your home in Me and so that I might heap blessings upon you. This is love." *('He and I', by Gabrielle Bossis p. 57)*

"How lovely is your dwelling place, O Lord of hosts
My soul longs and yearns for your courts
And my heart and flesh sing for joy to the living God.
One day in your presence Lord is far better to me than gold or to live my whole life somewhere else.

And I would rather be a door keeper in your
house than to take my fate upon myself.
You are my sun and my shield;
You're my lover from the start,
And the highway to God's city
runs through my heart.
(Composer unknown)

"From the moment you wake
Intercede for others.
Claim sinners for Me.
You cannot note the joy
you would give Me.
I died for them.
If you don't help Me today,
I won't be able to save this soul or that one
and you know I love them.
Then save them, as though you were saving
Me." *('He and I' by Gabrielle Bossis, p. 55)*

We have a lovely custom of lighting candles
in Church for those for whom we wish to
pray; or if we have a special intention, we
like to mark our prayer of petition to God,
by leaving a candle burning while we go
about our daily life. This custom, helps us
to remember the Lord's 'special' Presence
in the Catholic Church, and His loving care
for us and our needs throughout the day. It
is a lovely custom.

PSALM TWENTY THREE

While this candle is
burning, O Lord!

Let this candle that I light here,
be the light that leads me in my
many difficulties and decisions.
Let it be the Fire that
burns all selfishness,
pride and impurity in me.
Let it be the Flame
that warms my heart.
I cannot stay long in
this Your house.
By letting this candle burn,
It is part of myself
I want to give to You.
Help me to carry on my prayer
in today's activities.

(Anonymous)

A revelation to Charles de Foucauld on 4th Sunday of Lent 1898, Ephraim:

'(Our Lord): I am the Good Shepherd, I am tireless in My search for the lost sheep. I have told you so a hundred times: *Love Me!* Because I have shown such love for you, all of you, my sheep, love one another because your Shepherd loves you all so tenderly!... Be grateful to Me for how I look for you. For My goodness in forgiving you. For my joy when I find you. *Help Me in my work, do as I do.* Do all you can, with Me and like Me, each according to the advice of his spiritual director, to bring as many lost sheep back as possible... share My thoughts, My sorrow at seeing My sheep wander off, My joy at finding them ... share My perseverance; My hope, My indulgence in looking for them, My hope which never rejects the possibility of their return; My indulgence in forgiving them ... share My tenderness for them when they come back... far from reproaching and punishing them, I clasp them in My arms and kiss them tenderly, as the father did to his prodigal son.

So that all souls living in this world will come back to the path of goodness, work for this within the limits of obedience, and

be *tender* to sinners who return, as you
have seen Me to be to so many souls … In
short, *do for sinners what you would want
Me to do for you.'*
(*Charles de Foucauld, 'Ecrits spirituels', pp.167-8*)

"Even if they don't know what to call Me,
Let them tell Me of their tenderness
without giving Me any name.
Pray for those who are afraid.
How can they be?
How could anyone be afraid of such a Good
Shepherd ?
Even the very little lambs climb on His
knees and rest there.
And this is the Shepherd's joy!"
(*'He and I,' by Gabrielle Bossis, p. 151*)

*This popular Poem 'Sheep and Lambs' is
often sung by choral societies.*

All in the April evening,
April airs were abroad;
The sheep with their little lambs
Passed me by on the road.

The sheep with their lambs
Passed me by on the road;
All in the April evening
I thought on the Lamb of God.

The lambs were weary with crying
With a weak, human cry.
I thought of the Lamb of God
Going gently to die.

Up in the blue, blue mountains
Dewy pastures are sweet;
Rest for the little bodies,
Rest for the little feet.

But for the Lamb of God,
Up on the hill-top green,
Only a Cross of shame
Two stark crosses between.

All in the April evening,
April airs were abroad;
I saw the sheep with their lambs,
And thought on the Lamb of God.
(Katharine Tynan, b.1861)

Jesus, the Good Shepherd, was called the
'Lamb of God' by His cousin, John the
Baptist. In giving His life for His sheep,
Jesus became the Sacrificial Lamb of God,
who died to take away the sins of the world.
He now reigns victorious in Heaven at His
Father's right hand. *(cf. Hebrews 12:2)*
When our Blessed Mother appeared in
Knock in the west of Ireland, she came with
the Lamb of God on the altar of Sacrifice.

"In my vision, I heard the sound of an immense number of angels gathered round the throne and the animals and the elders; there were ten thousand times ten thousand of them and thousands upon thousands, shouting, 'the Lamb that was sacrificed is worthy to be given power, riches, wisdom, strength, honour, glory and blessing.'

Then I heard all the living things in creation – everything that lives in the air, and on the ground, and under the ground, and in the sea, crying, 'To the One who is sitting on the throne and to the Lamb, be all praise, honour, glory and power, for ever and ever'. And the four animals said, 'Amen'; and the elders prostrated themselves to worship." *(Revelation 5:11-14)*

And by the way, did you know that God is Transcendent? The Book of Revelation, at the end of time, will open up to us the Vision of the Divine Transcendence, the Vision of the Beyond:

"The things that no eye has seen and no ear has heard, things beyond the mind of man, all that God has prepared for those who love Him." (1 Corinthians 2:9)

Then the Veil will be lifted, and we will see God face to face.

THE END

POSTSCRIPT!

I hope you will continue to enjoy this book and I hope, too, that it will have helped you as much as it continues to help me.

It was a gift from Heaven, and like all gifts, it can either be accepted or refused; loved or unloved; treasured or discarded; used or not used; studied or ignored. To those who receive it with an 'open mind', it will bring undreamed of transformation and happiness.

If you have enjoyed it, and you haven't read the parent book 'God's Whistle", I suggest that you treat yourself to a copy and delve into that too!

The theme of Inner Healing pervades both books, and the use of God's Word is imperative in both! Many lives have been restored, healed through the fervent use of 'God's Whistle', and I often receive letters of gratitude, thanking me for writing it. But in both cases, I have only been the pen to put on paper what the Heavenly Author dictated!

ACKNOWLEDGEMENTS

My sincere thanks to all our benefactors who have made this book possible, and to the people who have helped it to be produced so quickly:–

to Paul Pearson and Christine Scotcher, for their invaluable and helpful suggestions and proof reading;
to my community for their support and encouragement;
to Séan and Ann O'Connor for their constant vigilance and support;
to Judy and Stephen Fox and Gerald Vann, for their lovely photographs;
to The Carmelite Monastery, Quidenham, for use of photographs;
to artist Terry Harrison and his wife, for kind permission to use their gorgeous watercolour painting 'Tranquil Waters';
to artists Peter and Gunvor Edwards and son Per, for use of their lovely drawing of the 'Shepherd and Dog';
to Fr. Augustine Aoun, for his giving prompt availability of the Aramaic version of Psalm 23; for Stephen Wilson's Psalm 23;
to The Bath Press, Bath, for a perfect job.

To all and everyone, God bless you always.

I have diligently sought copyright permission for everything in this book.

My sincere thanks to all:– to C.T.S. , for permission to quote from 'Abide with us, Lord' and 'Give yourself to Christ'; to Darton, Longman and Todd for permission to use paragraphs from 'Silent Pilgrimage to God' by Charles de Foucauld, published D.L.T., 1974 G.B.; for permission to use paragraphs from 'In Search of the Beyond' by Carlo Carretto, 1975 G.B.; to Mediaspaul, Canada, for kindest permission to use extracts from 'He and I' by Gabrielle Bossis, available at www.heandi.qc.ca; to The Grail, England, for permission to use the setting of Psalm 23; to Palphot, Israel, for photo of 'Shepherd and Herd' graciously donated: Permission is sought for 'All times are His Seasons' by John Donne; for photo of Pope John Paul II with Cardinal Wyszynski; for the words of 'Amazing Grace' by John Newton; for the words of 'All in an April Evening' by Katharine Tynan; for 'Psalm 23' by George Herbert. All copyrights have been sought. I shall put any omission right in my next edition.

HEALING TAPES and CD's

Please send me your singing tapes or CD's

- ☐ ..... copies **Songs of the Heart**
- ☐ ..... copies **Circle of Love**
- ☐ ..... copies **Beyond the Christmas Tree**
- ☐ ..... copies **Inner Healing & Healing of Memories** (Talk)

In addition to this book 'Near Restful Waters' there are other titles available:-

'God's Whistle' (– the Parent book)

4 Mini pocket sized versions:–

'A Call to Awareness'

'A Call to Forgive'

'A Call to Inner Healing'

'A Call to Being'

13 Aspreys, Olney, Bucks, MK46 5LN, U.K.
Tel: 01234-712162 * Fax: 01234-241995

I am always ready to receive a letter or telephone call from you and to pray there and then for any special needs you might have.   There's no charge or subscription to join **our Prayer Circle.**   There is great strength in knowing that you are not on your own. Together with our Community of the Daughters of the Holy Spirit, I pray for all the Members of the Prayer Circle every day.

Your Surname … … … … … … … … …

Christian Name … … … … … … … … …

Address … … … … … … … … … … …

Post Code …………… Tel: ………………